Arthur Edward Waite, Pietro Antonio Boni, Giano Lacinio

The New Pearl of Great Price

A Treatise Concerning the Treasure and Most Precious Stone of the Philosophers

Arthur Edward Waite, Pietro Antonio Boni, Giano Lacinio

The New Pearl of Great Price
A Treatise Concerning the Treasure and Most Precious Stone of the Philosophers

ISBN/EAN: 9783337069926

Printed in Europe, USA, Canada, Australia, Japan

Cover: Foto ©Thomas Meinert / pixelio.de

More available books at **www.hansebooks.com**

THE NEW PEARL OF GREAT PRICE.

THE NEW PEARL OF GREAT PRICE.

A TREATISE CONCERNING THE TREASURE
AND MOST PRECIOUS STONE OF
THE PHILOSOPHERS.

OR THE METHOD AND PROCEDURE OF THIS DIVINE ART;
WITH OBSERVATIONS DRAWN FROM THE WORKS OF
ARNOLDUS, RAYMONDUS, RHASIS, ALBERTUS,
AND MICHAEL SCOTUS, FIRST PUBLISHED
BY JANUS LACINIUS, THE CALABRIAN,
WITH A COPIOUS INDEX.

THE ORIGINAL ALDINE EDITION TRANSLATED INTO ENGLISH.

London:
JAMES ELLIOTT AND CO.,
TEMPLE CHAMBERS, FALCON COURT, FLEET STREET, E.C.
1894.

ANALYSIS OF CONTENTS.

	PAGE.
Preface to the English Translation	vii.
The Epigrams of Pierius Roseus and Hippolytus Fantolius Delphicus	1
The Greeting of Janus Lacinius, the Calabrian Minorite Friar	4
Nuncupatory Discourse	8
A Form and Method of Perfecting Base Metals, by Janus Lacinius	21
The New Pearl of Great Price	49
The Epistle of Bonus	298
Extracts made by Lacinius from the Works of Arnoldus de Villa Nova	305
Epitome of the Work of Raymondus Lullius	350
Extracts from the Light of Lights by Rhasis	365
Extracts from Albertus Magnus, S. Thomas, and other Sages	389
Curious Investigation concerning the Nature of the Sun and Moon, from Michael Scotus	417
Analytical Table of Contents	429

PREFACE
TO THE ENGLISH TRANSLATION.

TWO features of special interest attach to the "Pearl of Great Price," as written by Bonus of Ferrara, and edited by Janus Lacinius. In the first place, it is one of the earliest works printed on alchemy, and the original is a very beautiful specimen of typography. Concerning the latter point, it is only necessary to say that it was issued from the press of Aldus, appearing in 1546, with the privilege of Pope Paul III. and the Senate of Venice for the space of ten years. This edition is, of course, exceedingly rare, and is highly prized by collectors. In the second place, it is a very clear, methodical, and well-reasoned treatise, comparing favourably in these respects with the bulk of alchemical literature. A reader who is unacquainted with alchemy will probably not appreciate these points, but any one who, like the present editor, has had occasion to become widely familiar with Hermetic authors, will do honour to the lucidity of Bonus.

Concerning the adept himself, no biographical materials whatsoever are forthcoming, nor, as in most other cases, is there even a legend to fall back on. He is supposed to have been a native of Lombardy, and to have performed his alchemical labours at Pola, a maritime town of Istria, about 1330. He is sometimes described as Bonus of Ferraria,* and on this and other grounds Tiraboschi † identifies him with the "monk Ferarius," who about the same period

---

* And also of Traguria in Dalmatia, Mantua, and other places.

† Storia della Letturatura Italiana, Tom. V., Part I., p. 332. This work attacks Lenglet du Fresnoy, the historian of alchemy, as an inexact writer, but Tiraboschi had no acquaintance whatsoever with alchemy, and does not seem to have read the authors whom he endeavours to identify. Imaginative persons might, perhaps, be more inclined to question the equivocal name of Janus, the Calabrian Minorite Friar, and to suspect that his master Bonus was possibly his alter ego.

produced two treatises, namely, *De Lapide Philosophorum* and *Thesaurus Philosophiæ*, which are printed in the *Theatrum Chemicum*. A comparison of these works, which, unlike the *Pretiosa Margarita*, are exceedingly obscure, and have been at no time esteemed by students,* does not seem to justify this course.

The original manuscript upon which the monk of Calabria laboured, does not seem to have been published. The work which is attributed to Bonus, under the title of *Introductio in Divinam Chemiæ Artem Integram*, which appeared in quarto at Basle, and is reprinted

---

* Nous avons aussi le Traité du Moine Efferari ou Ferrari, mais ce dernier est peu lû par les connoisseurs : quoiqu'au milieu de beaucoup d'obscurité on y trouve quelques rayons de lumière, mais qu'il faut y savoir découvrir. On le croit de la fin du treizième siècle, ou du moins du commencement du quatorzième, parce qu'en citant Geber, La Tourbe, et le solitaire Morien, il ne dit pas un mot d'Arnaud de Villeneuve, ni de Raymond Lulle ; c'étoient cependant deux grands maîtres, qui méritoient bien d'être citées, s'il avoit vécu après eux.—*Historie de la Philosophie Hermétique.*—It may also be noted that these authors are not cited by Bonus, who quotes incessantly, but at the same time from a very limited circle of the most ancient Sages.

in the *Theatrum Chemicum* as well as in the collection of Mangetus, is simply the *Pearl of Great Price* * under another title; but we have also *Petri Boni de Secreto Omnium Secretorum Dei Dono Liber*, in 8vo, Venitiis, 1564.

The abridgment of the *Pretiosa Margarita*, made by Janus Lacinius, has received the reputation of fidelity on the faith of the editor's claim, and, in the absence of the original, it would be neither wise nor benevolent to dispute it. It is, however, of unmanageable length, and abounds, after the fashion of the period, in prolix disquisitions upon side issues, so that in the present translation it has been found necessary to abridge the abridgment, and to present the English reader with a faithful digest which omits nothing of importance, but presents it in an accessible form, by a

---

* There are various editions of the *Pretiosa Margarita Novella*, under one or other of its titles—as, for example, that of Basle, 4to, 1572; that of Argentoratum, 8vo, 1608; an 8vo is catalogued by bibliographers, without name of place, under date 1692. A German translation appeared at Leipsic, in 1714.

reasonable and patient pruning of mere repetitions and irrelevances. Those who are unskilled in the Latin that was written by alchemists will, it is hoped, take this statement on trust, and will extend to the present editor the courtesy that was dispensed to Lacinius by bibliographers like Lenglet du Fresnoy. On the other hand, the student who will be at the pains to compare this version with the Aldine original, will, it is also hoped, be justified in endorsing the claim.

ARTHUR EDWARD WAITE.

EPIGRAM,

ADDRESSED TO THE GENTLE READER BY PIERIUS ROSEUS.

THIS work casts out cruel disease from the human body, disease produced by malignant humours; and thus you are preserved. It will teach you how to regain the beautiful flower of youth, and how to secure a green and placid old age. All this may be yours, by the favour of the gods. Poverty will be triumphantly put to flight; your treasure-house will be filled; you will be able to succour the needy, and to render the sacrifice of praise to great Jupiter.

ANOTHER EPIGRAM, BY THE SAME.

Those who, for the sake of gain, have endured all manner of toil, our Calabrian bids be of a good heart. Do you love the goldmaker's art? Surprise and ecstasy are in store for you! But if any man do not possess this book, let him not dream that he can attain anything.

AN EPIGRAM

IN HENDECASYLLABIC LINES,

BY HIPPOLYTUS FANTOTIUS DELPHICUS, OF PERUSINUS.

I, the Divine Art, having long suffered indignity at the hands of foolish impostors, lay sorrowing in thick darkness. Then did I imploringly beseech illustrious men of learning to pity my doleful plight, and to succour my distress; but my suppliant hands were uplifted in vain. At last one of them was filled with compassion because of my moans and tears; Lacinius flung wide my prison doors, and set a lordly crown on my head. By the flashing light of genius, he shewed to all what glorious rewards I had to bestow on my followers; and every reader may see what stores of wisdom and learning I showered upon him. All the knowledge of Geber, of Bonus, and all which Raymond signified in so many books, the power of his genius focussed in one small treatise. Worthy of the highest honour is this illustrious Master, whose teaching renders me accessible to all men.

JANUS LACINIUS, THE CALABRIAN MINORITE FRIAR (OF PSYCHRONEA), TO THE GENTLE READER SENDS GREETING.

THE philosophers inform us that opposites belong to the same category, and therefore they throw light on each other by being brought into juxtaposition. The illustrious character of liberality and generosity only intensifies the disgrace of avarice and selfish greed. Those who know that life was bestowed on them for the sake of their friends and their country, whose years also are spent in the service of others, are worthy of the most distinguished honour. Those, on the other hand, who, by the pride of life and the greed of gain, are led to bury their talents, and to turn a deaf ear to the appeals of justice and humanity, while they avariciously and relentlessly pursue their own selfish pleasure, are such vile, abandoned, and harpy-like creatures that they are justly branded with the contempt and execration of mankind. The despicable avarice of those who, so far from doing any good with their money to others, do not even enjoy it themselves, by its hateful and repulsive want of social kindness sets off to the greatest advantage the overflowing generosity and liberality of opposite natures. Hence, after my return from Cisalpine Gaul to Padua, I was greatly attracted by a most lucid discourse of Bonus, a profound scholar of Ferrara, on the possibility and truth of the Alchemistic Art. Concerning this subject, he expressed himself with such profound, subtle, copious, and accurate learning that I cannot remember any obscure point which was not touched upon with unprecedented clearness and definiteness. This dissertation must be of the greatest utility, not only to ardent students of Alchemy, but even to its detractors. I should, therefore, be justly chargeable with meanness and illiberality if I refused to do all in my power to make it accessible to the general public. Such an accusation I should be loth indeed to incur, and I have, therefore, arranged for the publication of the aforesaid memorable discourse of Bonus of Ferrara, together with copious extracts from the works of Raymondus Lullius, Arnold of Villanova, Michael Scotus, Rhasis, Albertus, and other men of light and leading. In this synopsis you will find nothing that is not profound, excellent, and positively reliable. The Sages whom I have quoted possess so remarkable an insight into the nature of things, so abundant and incredible a store of learning, that solemn importance attaches to every word they utter; but it is my opinion that Bonus excels them all, and I am sure that the reader will agree with me when he sees the golden current of philosophy issue from his lips. He is more profound than all the rest in laying the foundations of his system, more subtle in his manner of expressing truth, more lucid in setting forth the secret working of Nature. It is my admiration for his genius that has induced me to describe his discourse as a "Pearl of Great Price." The pearls which we find here are indeed precious, without an obscuring spot, but clear and pure, utterly unlike the writings of those who only embarrass and bewilder the enquirer by their dark and hopelessly perplexing phraseology. Our Bonus sheds noonday brightness where they dispense only darkness as of Egypt: he shews to all students not only the truth and possibility, but the actual necessity of our Art. His utterances I have, with great industry, collected, elucidated, and expurgated, and I here present them to the student in an accessible form. Accept my gift with a joy proportioned to its worth; fold it close to your heart; thank God for it; read it diligently, day and night; and accept my best wishes that it may lead you onward to success. If this book be well received, I intend to follow it up with an explanatory synopsis of all the works of Raymondus Lullius. Farewell.

Nuncupatory Discourse,
the Interlocutors being Lacinius and Bonus, of Ferrara.

Bonus. It is both customary and right, O Lacinius, that those who have accomplished anything worth mentioning in any art or science should make known their discoveries to the world, in order that mankind at large may be benefited by them. This office I have not been able to perform for myself; but as you have collected and studied my works, I earnestly hope that you will not suffer them to remain covered with the dust of forgetfulness, but that you will send me forth, in company with Arnold, Raymond, and others, to deliver my message to mankind.

Lacinius. I will gladly do what you ask. But there is a time-honoured custom amongst authors of dedicating their works to some Pope or Prince whose favour they wish to gain, or whose patronage they desire to acknowledge. To whom shall your book be dedicated?

Bonus. I am aware of the custom which you mention. Some adopt this device in order to save their work from the obscurity and neglect which they may have good reason to fear. Others, by placing the name of some illustrious person on the title-page, desire to safeguard themselves against the supercilious carelessness of critics, who at once throw aside any book of which the author is as yet unknown to fame. Thus, in dedicating their writings to great men, most authors are impelled by motives of self-interest, for they know very well that their patrons will probably never so much as look at their production. For this and other reasons, I do not wish my book to be dedicated to either Pope or Prince.

Lacinius. But are you not afraid of the insolence of the envious, the abuse of the greedy, the sneers of sciolists, the calumnies of merchants—in short, the opposition of all who think that nobody is wise but themselves? Will not their enmity shroud you in Cimmerian darkness?

Bonus. It is the nature of curs to bark, and they will do so while they live, especially when they see any one better than themselves. I do not care what fools say, but only what honest men, and what truth itself, may utter.

Lacinius. But if I dedicate you to some illustrious Prince they will perhaps cease to bark.

Bonus. You take too favourable a view of these men. If their mouths are filled with blasphemy against God, we cannot expect them to reverence anything. No, do not let any hope of propitiating them change your purpose.

Lacinius. But, perhaps, a patron might reward me for my labour, and thus enable me to live.

Bonus. So thought Aurelius Augurellus, who dedicated his work on gold-making to Pope Leo X., and received from that prelate, whose generosity was well-known, a gown of green silk, the colour of hope.

Lacinius. He was right. For how could he give anything more costly to a man who professed to be an adept in the art of gold-making? Might I not at least shew my gratitude to some old and dear friends and benefactors by inscribing the work to them?

Bonus. By such a course you would be more likely to convert your friends into enemies. Do you not know that all who practise this art are very anxious to keep it a secret from the whole world?

Lacinius. Alas! Is it, then, a profane pursuit?

Bonus. That is the opinion of the vulgar. But the art is sacred, and all its adepts are sanctified and pure. For "men either discover it because they are holy, or it makes them holy."

Lacinius. That is not the opinion of the present age. People say that this art is unbecoming not only a godly but even an honest man.

Bonus. And do you also echo the ignorant babble of the vulgar?

Lacinius. Would it were of the vulgar only! But I know that it is the opinion of all classes, both high and low, learned and ignorant.

Bonus. Can it be true? Surely they must be thinking of those sophistical impostors who are a disgrace to our science. Such men are not philosophers, but thieves and robbers: between us and them there is all the difference of day and night, good and evil, God and mammon. But, nevertheless, by their wicked and shameless practices, they have succeeded in making our blessed Art a byword among the vulgar. Yet it is essentially an art which can never become known to any but honest and god-fearing persons. Was not the inventor of this Art, the thrice-great Hermes, a person of signal sanctity? Are there not among the professors of the great magistery holy divines like John of Damascus, Albertus Magnus, S. Thomas, Roger Bacon, Haymon, Raymond, Godfrey, John, the most reverend Bishop of Ticina, Cardinal Garsia, Friar Helyas, Friar William, Friar Richard, Peter of Iliacum, Morienus, and many other monks, nay, as Vincentius, the historian, tells us, S. John the Evangelist himself? Of the latter it is said that when the two youths, who had given all their goods to the poor for the sake of Christ, were heavy at heart because they saw their slaves arrayed in gorgeous robes, while they themselves were poorly clad, he bade them bring him bundles of rods and pebbles from the seashore, and changed them all into pure gold. This, however, I regard as a miracle, rather than a proof of our Art, for the substance was too unlike that which we use, and "one action does not make an artist." But what shall I say of Raymond, whose life and genius are the admiration of all? Raymond was first opposed to this magistery, and attempted to convince

Arnold de Villanova of its impossibility, but was himself overcome, not so much in argument as by the evidence of his senses. By this discomfiture, Raymond was induced to study the Art; and when his search was crowned with success, he became the foremost champion of Alchemy, writing 500 volumes in its defence. He was also the first to discover the method of evolving precious stones out of the metallic principles; nay, he was able, not only to change lead into gold, but he transmuted gold into lead, and thus turned back the course of Nature. It is also related of him that he performed the almost incredible task of transmuting a tiny bar of metal partly into gold, partly into silver, brass, tin, iron, and lead. Are these things of no account? Are they absurd or ridiculous? And is it not wicked and unworthy of a refined and cultivated mind to suppose that the knowledge and practice of our Art is unbecoming a religious and god-fearing man? If Paul wove tents, if Luke painted, and Peter and John pursued the calling of fishermen, honest and useful work cannot be unworthy the attention of a godly person. Surely, it is more religious to do something than to be idle!

Lacinius. Your argument is unanswerable, for you appeal to the practice of those whose words and deeds were the standard of truth, justice, faith, innocence, religion, and holiness for all mankind: as the sky is illumined with stars, so they were appointed as the lights of the world.

Bonus. Why, then, are you so fearful of launching our little book without any dedicatory inscription?

Lacinius. I fear most that this book may make the matter too clear to the vulgar herd, thus bestowing God's most precious earthly gift upon the wicked and undeserving, in defiance of the ancient precept.

Bonus. That rule was more applicable to men of old than to our present state of Christian liberty. Heathen Sages might be fearful of spreading this knowledge too commonly, but Christ has taught us the true use of riches—to relieve the wants of the poor and needy.

Lacinius. Why, then, do our masters follow in the footsteps of the ancients, and predict ruin to mankind from the "profanation" of this mystery? John de Rupescissa conjures his readers not to make the Art known to the wicked and unbelieving, as such a course would ruin the Christian faith.

Bonus. Do you imagine that the faith of Jesus Christ, the Son of God, can be overthrown by these means? Has it not always grown most rapidly, precisely where it has been most severely opposed? But Christ Himself has given us a sovereign rule for our guidance in this matter: "Freely ye have received, freely give." What is the use of concealed diamonds, or a hidden treasure, to the world? What is the use of a lighted candle if it be placed under a bushel? It is the innate selfishness of the human heart which makes these persons seek a pious pretext for keeping this knowledge from mankind.

Lacinius. I know some men who are so jealous of the preservation of this secret that they will hardly read their own books, and would not for all the world allow any one else to look at them, just as if they feared that the Stone would at once leap forth from the book, if it were only opened, and that it would soon lie about in every gutter. These persons are such skinflints withal that they would rather remain in ignorance than spend a single penny in search of the Stone. I suppose they expect the knowledge to be showered down upon them from heaven. Surely we have reason to pray that such people may be delivered from their own blinding meanness and illiberality.

Bonus. Would that a ray of Divine light might illumine the gross darkness of their understandings! But I am afraid that their folly is past praying for. If indeed they could be brought to see that this world is under Divine rule and governance, that no mortal can approach God but by God, that even the light cannot be perceived without light, they might come to understand that, without the special grace of God, this ineffable gift is not bestowed on any man.

Lacinius. How can those harpies reply to that argument?

Bonus. They are in a state of frenzied ignorance, which prevents them from perceiving the difficulties of the task; and so the Stone which they find is the Stone of Sisyphus. For "they are few whom Jupiter loves, or whom their manly perfection exalts to the stars." When, indeed, the Stone is found, our friends, who now laugh and sneer at us, will be at a loss how to express their love.

Lacinius. Alas, that this glorious and heavenly magistery should be regarded by many as a mere fraud and imposture!

Bonus. No wonder, if overweening and ignorant persons such as carpenters, weavers, smiths, take upon themselves to set up laboratories, and to pretend to a knowledge of our Art. The universal prevalence of impostors naturally makes people think that our whole Art is a fraud from beginning to end.

Lacinius. But is this knowledge not also sought by learned men, nobles, princes, and even by kings?

Bonus. Yes, but the motive which prompts them all is an illiberal love of gold. Their hearts are as hard as the flints which they wish to change into the precious metals, and they are as ignorant withal of the elementary facts of Nature as the poorest labourer. The consequence is that they fall an easy prey to impostors and itinerant charlatans, and spend their lives in foolishly experimenting with arsenic, sulphur, and all manner of solvents. Thus, instead of learning to prepare the Stone, they dissipate their money, and have empty pockets for their pains.

Lacinius. It is a just reward for their folly; for what have those substances to do with metals?

Bonus. We will then send forth our little book, not protected with the name of any prince or noble, but equipped only with the strength of virtue and truth, after the manner of those Egyptian kings who dedicated all things to Mercury, the giver of virtue and genius, and to the Sun, the generator of all things. We will dedicate our book to Mercury and the Sun, and to all who love righteousness and truth. But those wise people who do not approve of anything that they do not understand must listen to the book, and let it speak for itself. It is well for an author if he has no need to commend himself, because his book commends him. He were a vain workman who looked for praise and preferment from anything but the value of his work. Farewell.

A Form and Method of Perfecting Base Metals,

by Janus Lacinius Therapus, the Calabrian.

The art of Generating M or Q.

SOME of the principles of our Art are apprehended mentally or intellectually, such as Chaos, Alteration, Power, Operation, Generation, and Digestion. Others are perceived by the senses, as wine, or the First Matter, body or form, elements, the perfect being, the forming ferment, colours, fermentation, separation. Some are apprehended both by mind and sense, *e.g.*, Sky, or Heaven.

A. From CHAOS goes forth an intelligent Master, who, amidst the rude, confused, and undigested mass of the elements, perceives himself advancing towards M or Q, until by B, C, D, and by the primordial elements, which follow from Nature herself, he arrives thither.

B. The SUBSTANCE is that from which D arises when the Artificer works extrinsically. We also apply it to the imperfect metals which are to be changed into M or Q.

C. The FORM is the intelligent outward influence (the Master), which, sets in motion these Principles. It is that also which gives being to M or Q, and by which T, S, V, Z are changed into X or Y.

D. The Sky is the female principle, by which that which is received of the male is nourished and increased until it is wholly changed into M or Q.

E. The ELEMENTS are changed from B into D, and by way of C, on the other hand, F, G, H, I, are intermingled.

F. CONVERSION takes place, first of C into D, and then of D into C, finally of both in turn into M or Q. F also indicates the potency of which

D is the Act, and through which pearls are made and generated artificially.

G. PERMIXTION is the union of the male and the female principle (*e.g.*, C with D).

H. DISSOLUTION is the hermaphroditic conception which takes place in either C or D.

I. GENERATION is partly that by which C and D produce M, and partly that by which M and D produce Q. If we place the Substance in a closed vessel, it is brought about by Nature rather than by the aid of art.

K. Of COLOURS, the first is black, which is more difficult to bring about than the rest, from the fact that it is the first. It shews that C and D have united, and that conception has taken place, *i.e.*, that M or Q will ultimately be produced. Then comes white, by which we gradually progress from C to M, and thence to Q; then saffron, which indicates that the conjunction of the substances is in progress, because the seed is diffused through the whole of D; the fourth colour is red, indicating the actual accomplishment of M or Q.

L. DIGESTION is the gradual development of that which is conceived, by gentle outward heat, *e.g.*, the evolution of M out of C and D, or of Q out of M and D.

O. SEPARATION is the severing of elements, which, originating from B and D, are also separated from the same.

P. OPERATION is either the whole process of change by which B and the rest of the principles become M or Q, or the use of M and Q in transmuting base metals into silver or gold.

M. The PERFECT BEING is the efficient cause, or the form of that into which C and D are changed by way of E, F, G, H, I, K, L, O, P, and has power to perfect imperfect metals.

N. FERMENTATION is the wonderful principle by which M is developed into Q. It is brought about by the bland warmth of a gentle fire. Thus M is still wanting in some of the most potent properties of Q, which is the perfect Tincture. Q is capable of unlimited extension, not only quantitatively, but qualitatively. If you can change M into Q, you can multiply and perfect Q indefinitely.

Q, then, is the formative tincture, consummately perfect, and consisting of the equilibrium of all the elements. Hence its virtue is far greater and more potent than that of M. It changes imperfect metals into silver or gold (X or Y), and it is an efficacious remedy for all mental and bodily disease in man, seeing that it expels all disturbing elements; it also makes and keeps men good and kindly disposed towards others. It is, finally, a sovereign cure of the weakness of old age.

Mix one part of gold (X) with twelve parts of Our Water; pound them small; place them in a moderately deep jar; set over it an alembic in the ordinary way; stop up the jar and the apertures of the alembic, up to the beak, with clay; let it dry thoroughly; place it on the oven (not immediately over the coals, but on the iron) in such a way that the whole jar shall be covered by it as far as the alembic, and let the aperture between jar and furnace be also sealed with clay. Then light the fire, and there will come oil into the alembic, together with the water, and will float on the water with an orange colour. Continue the fire till all the water is distilled; let it cool; remove the recipient; separate the oil from the water, and open the jar: you will find a hard, brittle, and pulverisable body. If you like, repeat the whole process, pouring the same or other water over the body; distil as before. The water that comes out will not be so much as at first, and if you repeat the process a third time, there will be hardly any water at all. The body that remains will be a blackish powder, which you calcine in the following way:

If the body be one ounce, pour over it three ounces of Mercury, and pound them together, thus producing an amalgam like butter. Then place it in a glass vessel, and stop up the apertures with clay on the outer side. Set it on a trivet over a gentle fire of three or four coals, stirring it all the time with a small wooden rod, and be careful to shut your mouth and nose, because the fumes are destructive to the teeth. Continue to stir till all the Mercury has disappeared, and there remains a subtle body of more intense blackness. Repeat this even to the third time, till the body is pulverised and intensely black. Then take it, place it in a smaller vessel, and pour on it as much of the aforesaid oil as will moisten it; close the vessel, and let it stand over a lamp; in three days the body will be dried, and it will begin to assume a whitish appearance. Pour on more oil as before; dry by the same fire, and the substance will exhibit an increased whiteness. Repeat the process up to the fourth time; the substance will then have turned of a dazzling whiteness, delicate as an orient pearl of the purest water. Then proceed with our ore, salt, and gum, which must become one. A gentle fire can do no harm, but the warmth of horsedung is better.

The blackness of the substance, when it appears, is not the blackness of ink, but a bright ebony colour. When it has been changed into whiteness, we must then look out for the appearance of the saffron hue, which will in no long time be followed by a most glorious ruby colour. Between the appearance of M (the white colour) and Q (the ruby colour) there should be an interval of thirty days, during which the heat of the fire should be slightly increased, and the vessel kept carefully closed. The substance will then be perfect, and you should carefully preserve it for your own use and that of your friends. One part of it will transmute 2,000 parts of any base metal into its own glorious nature.

To change one drachm of M into Q, add to it three ounces of D and one ounce of C. Subject the whole to gentle coction for thirty days, till it passes through K, after which you will behold perfect Q, round and red. When you have performed and accomplished all this, you may consider yourself as a great master; and you should render to the great and good God fervent and constant thanks for His unspeakable benefit. Thus I have bestowed upon you a gift, gentle reader, the vast value of which will be understood by generations to come.

S = lead.   X = gold.
T = tin.   Y = silver.
V = iron.   Z = bronze.

[Figures representing these seven metals.]

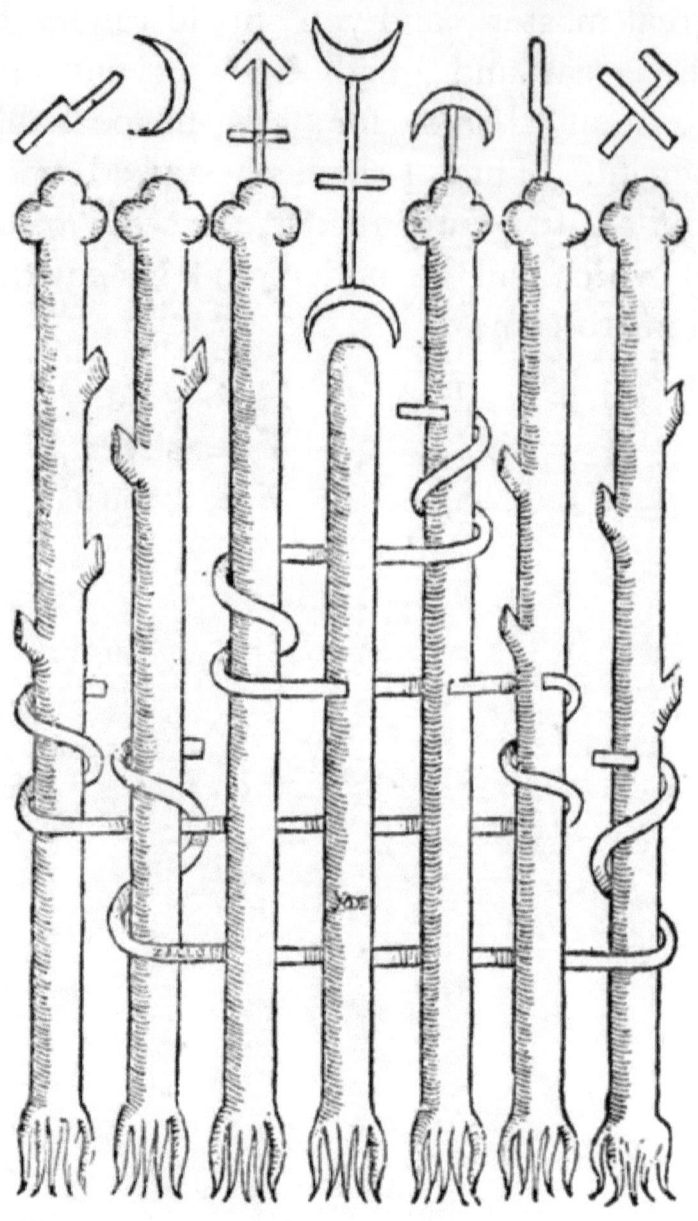

A Method of Perfecting Base Metals. 31

We have drawn the composition of the trees of the grove together; we will now describe their natures one by one, according to the best of our ability. We will, in the first place, begin with those trees upon the left, the scrolls whereof simply encircle the bark, and with their purgation as follows:—The first tree is hot, dry, red, like red-hot bronze. It becomes moist, dry, and black, like lead; cold and humid, like quicksilver; hot, humid, and saffron-coloured.

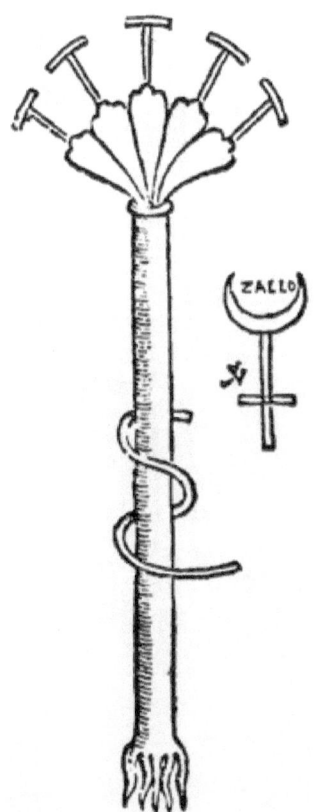

The second tree is hot and dry, like glowing brass; it becomes humid and black, like quicksilver; dry and white, like lead; hot, humid, and saffron-coloured, like blood-red gold.

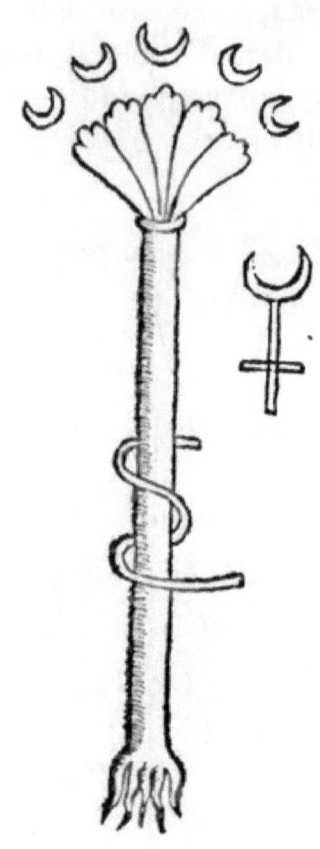

A Method of Perfecting Base Metals.

The third tree is hot, dry, and red. It becomes dry and black, like lead; humid and white, like tin or quicksilver; hot, humid, and saffron, like blood-red gold.

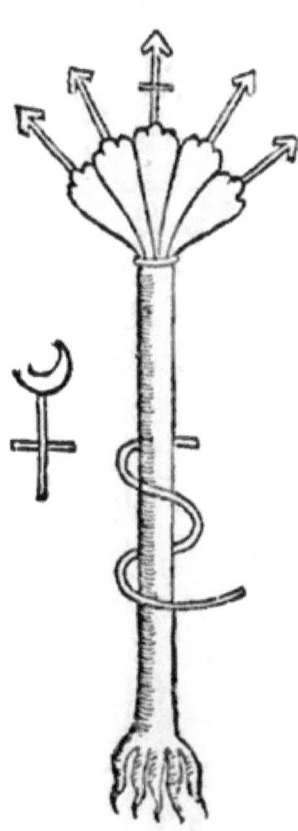

34 *The New Pearl of Great Price.*

The first tree on the right-hand side has a scroll which enters the front and comes out on the other side; it is hot, humid, and saffron-coloured, like red-hot gold. It becomes dry and black, like earthy silver; humid, like silver; hot, dry, and red, like red-hot bronze.

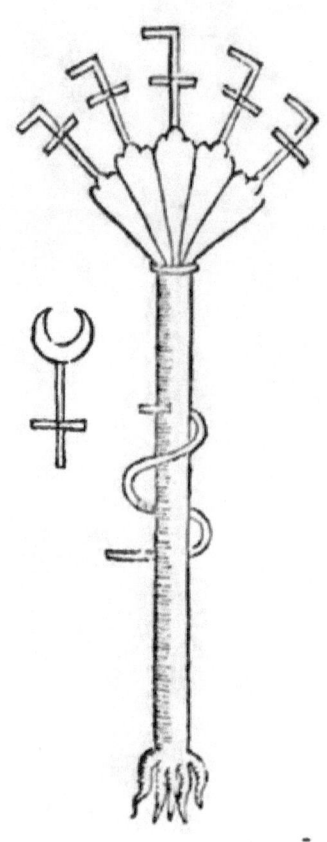

The second tree, which is pierced by its scroll, is dry and red, like red-hot bronze. It becomes dry and black, like lead; humid and white, like quicksilver; hot, humid, and saffron-coloured, like blood-red gold.

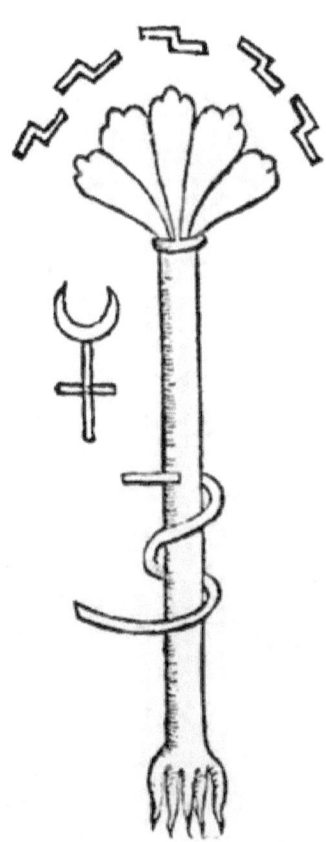

The third tree, which is pierced by its scroll, is hot, dry, and red, like red-hot bronze. It becomes dry and black, like lead; humid and white, like tin; hot, humid, saffron-coloured, and of a bloody red.

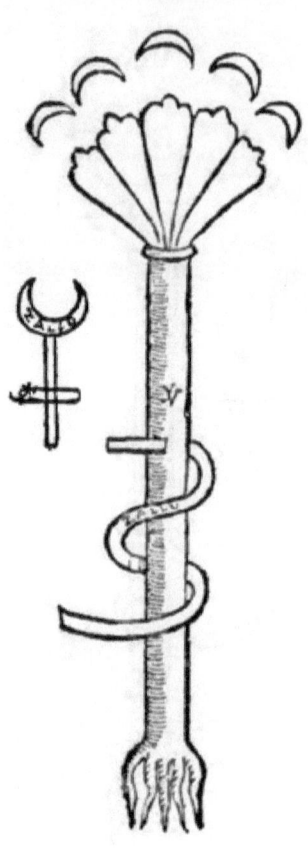

A Method of Perfecting Base Metals. 37

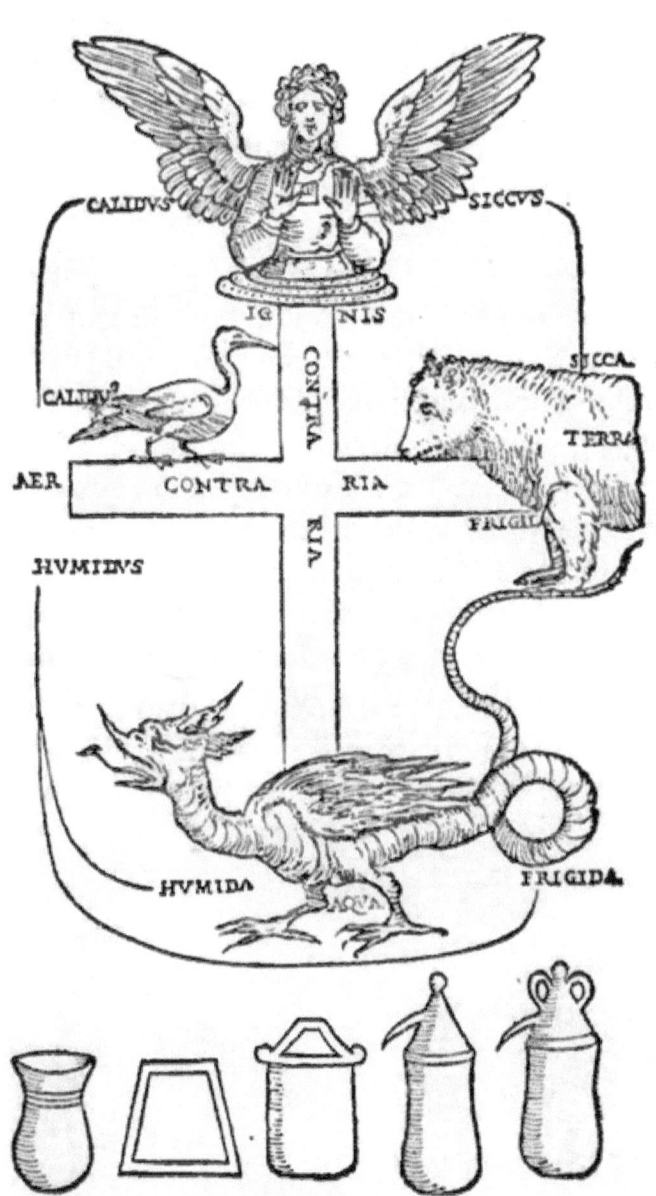

Exposition of the Typical Figures.

Three rules must be carefully observed in our art: first prepare the right substance; then carry on the work continuously, so that it may not be marred by interruption; thirdly, be patient, and follow always in the footsteps of Nature.

Get (as your substance) highly purified Water of Life, and keep it; but do not suppose that the liquid which moistens all things, is the bright and limpid liquid of Bacchus. For while you anxiously look about in out-of-the-way places for extraordinary events, you pass by the sparkling waves of the blessed stream.

Enter the Palace in which are fifteen mansions, where the king, his brow circled with the diadem, sits on a lofty throne, holding in his hand the sceptre of the whole world; before him, his son and five servants kneel in robes of different colours, imploring him to

bestow upon his son and his servants a share of his power; but he does not even reply to their request.

The son, incited by the servants, stabs the father as he sits on the throne. (Let an amalgam be made with highly purified water, etc.)

In the third picture we see the son catching his father's blood in his robe (which is the second process of our art, already explained in the method).

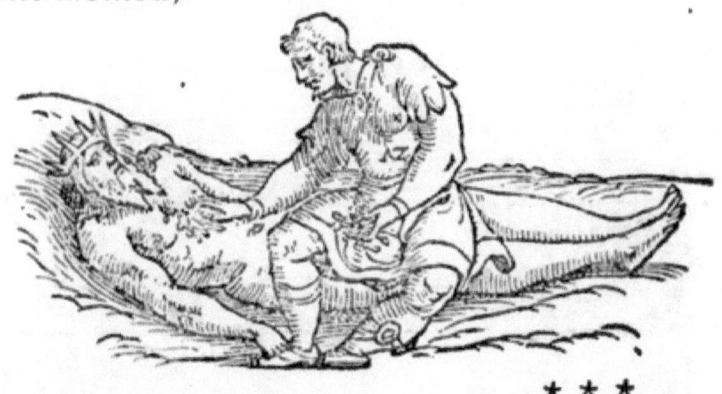

* * *

A grave is dug in the fourth mansion (which is the furnace). Its depth is two handbreadths, and its width four inches.

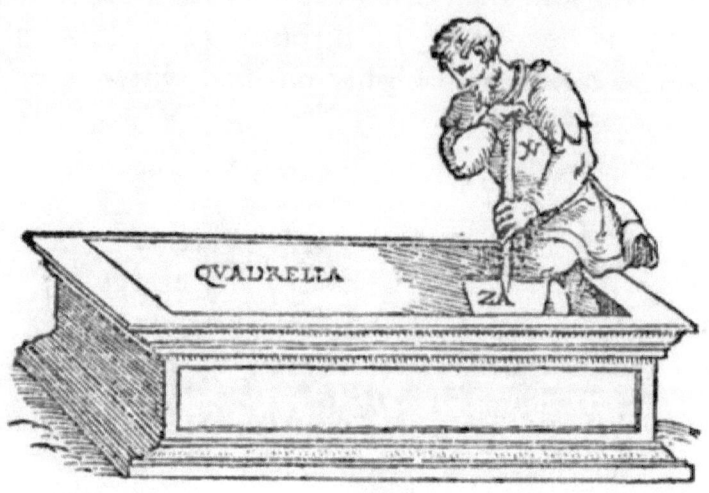

In the fifth mansion the son thought to throw his father into the grave, and to leave him there; but (by means of our art) both fell in together.

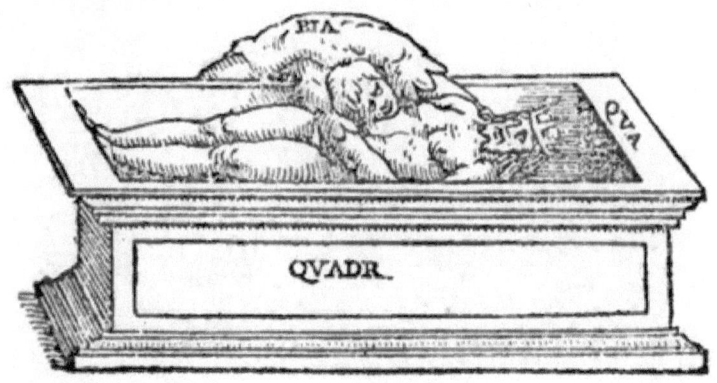

A Method of Perfecting Base Metals. 41

The sixth mansion is that in which the son still strives to get out, but one (who sprang from them in the second operation) comes, and prevents him from so doing.

While the father and son are in the tomb, which is called the seventh mansion, there follows putrefaction in their ashes, or a very hot bath.

In the eighth mansion, that which happened during the putrefaction is inspected, the vase having become cold, etc.

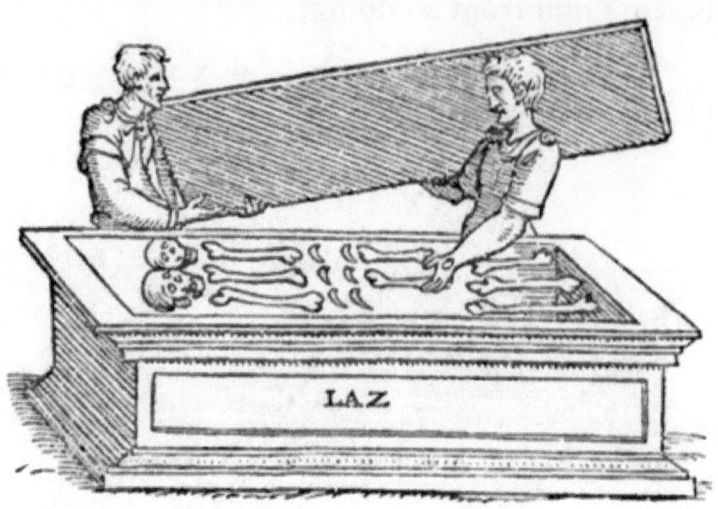

In the ninth mansion the bones are taken from the tomb. This happens when the whole body has been dissolved by successive solution, which, being done, keep it carefully.

A Method of Perfecting Base Metals. 43

In the tenth mansion, the bones are divided into nine parts, the dissolved substance being subjected to gentle coction for nine days, till a portion of it turns black. Remove this latter, and keep it in another vessel in a hot place. Subject the water to gentle heat for another nine days. Again remove that which has turned black, and put it with the rest. Continue the operation till the water is clear and pure. Let its Water of Life be poured over the black substance in a small glass vessel, so that it shall float over it to the height of an inch, and let it stand nine days over a gentle fire, renewing the water every day, if necessary. (Thus the earth will become clear and white, according to the teaching of the philosophers; for this earth is putrefied and purified with its water.)

An angel is sent, who casts the bones on the purified and whitened earth (which is now mixed with its seed, and let the whole be placed in a closed jar with its alembic. Let the thicker substance be divided from the water by a more violent fire, and remain as a hard substance at the bottom).

In the eleventh mansion the servants pray God to restore their king. Henceforth the whole work is concerned with his restoration.

A Method of Perfecting Base Metals.

For this purpose a second angel is sent in the twelfth mansion, who places the other part of those bones on the earth (till they are all thickened: then a wonderful thing happens).

Thus, a succession of angels is sent, who cast the first, second, third, and fourth part of the bones on the earth, where they become white, transparent, and firm. The fifth and sixth parts are changed into yellow, and so also with the seventh, eighth, and ninth; the earth of the bones becomes as red as blood or rubies.

Then the king rises from the tomb, full of the grace of God. His body is now all spiritual and heavenly, and he has power to make all his servants kings.

At last he exercises his power upon his servants and his son, placing crowns of gold upon their heads, and making them kings by his grace, since God had given him great power and majesty.

Let no impostor, greedy or wicked person, touch this glorious work with his unclean hands. Let the honest man and him of a wise heart come hither, and him who is capable of exploring the most hidden causes of things.

THE NEW PEARL OF GREAT PRICE,

Being a Concordance of the Sages on the Great Treasure, the Stone of the Philosophers, the Arcanum, the Secret of all Secrets, and the Gift of God.

BY PETER BONUS, OF FERRARA.

BOTH among ancients and moderns the question whether Alchemy be a real Art or a mere imposture has exercised many heads and pens; nor is it possible for us entirely to ignore the existence of such a dispute. A multiplicity of arguments has been advanced against the truth of our Art; but men like Geber and Morienus, who were best fitted to come forward in its defence, have disdained to answer the cavilling attacks of the vulgar. They have not, as a matter of fact, furnished us with anything beyond the bare assertion that the truth of

Alchemy is exalted beyond the reach of doubt. We will not follow their example, but, in order to get at the foundation of the matter, we will pass in review the arguments which have been, or may be, set forth on both sides of the question.

In the case of a science which is familiarly known to a great body of learned men, the mere fact that they all believe in it supersedes the necessity of proof. But this rule does not apply to the Art of Alchemy, whose pretensions, therefore, need to be carefully and jealously sifted. The arguments which make against the justice of those claims must be fairly stated, and it will be for the professors of the Art to turn back the edge of all adverse reasoning.

Every ordinary art (as we learn in the second book of the Physics) is either dispositive of substance, or productive of form, or it teaches the use of something. Our Art, however, does not belong to any one of these categories; it may be described indeed as both dispositive and productive, but it does not teach the use of anything. It truly instructs us how to know the one substance exclusively designed by Nature for a certain purpose, and it also acquaints us with the natural method of treating and manipulating this substance, a knowledge which may be either practically or speculatively present in the mind of the master. There are other crafts which are not artificial, but natural, such as the arts of medicine, of horticulture, and glass-blowing. They are arts in so far as they require an operator; but they are natural in so far as they are based upon facts of Nature. Such is the Art of Alchemy. Some arts systematise the creations of the human mind, as, for instance, those of grammar, logic, and rhetoric; but Alchemy does not belong to this class. Yet Alchemy resembles other arts in the following respect, that its practice must be preceded by theory and investigation; for before we can know how to do a thing, we must understand all the conditions and circumstances under which it is produced. If we rightly apprehend the cause or causes of a thing (for there often is a multiplicity or complication of causes), we also know how to produce that thing. But it must further be considered that no one can claim to be heard in regard to the truth or falsity of this Art who does not clearly understand the matter at issue; and we may lay it down as a rule that those who set up as judges of this question without a clear insight into the conditions of the controversy should be regarded as persons who are talking wildly and at random.

Reasons Apparently Militating against the Reality of our Art.

IT was usual among the ancients to begin with a destructive argument. This custom we will now follow.

Reason First.

Whoever is ignorant of the elements of which any given substance is composed, and of the quantities of each element in such composition, cannot know how to produce that substance. Now, the alchemists are necessarily ignorant of the exact composition of metals: therefore, as the metals are composite substances, it is not possible that the alchemists should know how to produce them.

Reason Second.

Again, if you are unacquainted with the determinate proportion of the elements entering into the composition of any given substance, you cannot possibly produce that substance. I allude to the exact degree of digestion which has taken place in, and the peculiar manner and mode of composition which constitute the specific essence, or form, of any assigned substance, and make it what it is. This specific form of metals can never become known to a human artist. It is one of Nature's own secrets, and the Art of Alchemy must, therefore, be pronounced not only unknowable, but utterly impossible.

Reason Third.

We are also ignorant of the proper or specific instrument, or means, which Nature uses to produce those peculiar substances defined as metals. We are aware that Nature, in the production of every different substance, uses a certain modified form of digestive heat. But in the case of metals, this digestive heat is not derived either from the sun, or, exclusively, from any central fire, for it is inextricably mixed and compounded of the two, and this in a manner which no man can imitate. Therefore, Alchemy is impossible.

Reason Fourth.

Moreover, we know that the generation of metals occupies thousands of years. This is the case in Nature's workshop in the bowels of the earth: hence we see that even if this Art were possible, man's life would not be long enough for its exercise. Everything requires for its generation a certain predetermined period of time; and we find in the case of animals and vegetables that this period of generation and development cannot be hastened to any considerable extent. It might indeed be said that Art can do in a month what Nature requires a thousand years to accomplish—by intensifying and exalting the temperature of the digestive warmth. But such a course would defeat its own object, since a greater degree of heat than is required for the development of metals (*i.e.*, an unnatural temperature) would hinder rather than accelerate that development.

Reason Fifth.

Again, the generation of metals, as of all things else, can only be accomplished in a certain place specially adapted to the purpose. Definite peculiar local conditions must be fulfilled if a seed is to spring up and grow; an animal can only be generated and developed in its own proper womb. Now, glass, stone, and earthenware jars and vessels can never take the place of the natural womb of metals in the bosom of the earth. Hence, Alchemy is nothing but a fraudulent pretence.

Reason Sixth.

Once more, that which is effected by Nature alone, cannot be produced artificially; and metals belong to this class of substances. Generation and corruption are the effect of an inward principle, and this inward principle is Nature, which creates the substantial forms of things. Art, on the other hand, is an outward principle, which can only bring about superficial changes.

Reason Seventh.

If Art cannot produce that which is of easy separation, and, therefore, of easy composition, it cannot produce that the separation and composition of which are more difficult. Now, a horse or a dog are easily decomposed, while the putrefaction of metals requires a great length of time. But yet Art cannot produce a horse or a dog; hence it can still less produce metals.

Reason Eighth.

Metals do indeed belong to the same genus or kind; they are all metals, just as a horse and a man are both animals. But as horse and man are specifically different, and as one species cannot be changed into another, so the various metals are specifically different; and as a dog can never become a man, so neither can one metal be changed into another. This reason and its solution are advanced by Geber.

Reason Ninth.

The principles which stir up the vital spark slumbering in metals are necessarily unknown to the student of Nature. For these principles are supplied by the movements and influences of the stars and heavenly bodies, which are overruled by the Supreme Intelligence, and preside over the generation, corruption, and conservation of species, imparting to everything its own peculiar form and perfection. These influences which determine whether a certain metallic substance shall be gold, silver, etc., no human mind can possibly fix or direct to any given spot. Therefore, etc.

Reason Tenth.

Artificial things bear the same relation to natural things which Art bears to Nature. But as Art is not Nature, neither are artificial things the same as natural things: and artificial gold, even if produced, would not be the same thing as natural gold. For the methods of Nature are inward, they are always one and the same, and never vary; but the methods of Art, on the other hand, vary with the idiosyncrasies of the artist.

Reason Eleventh.

It is easier to destroy than to make things: but we can hardly destroy gold: how then can we make it?

Reason Twelfth.

The ancient philosophers were in the habit of teaching all the arts and sciences they knew to their disciples, and of declaring them in their books; but of this Art they never mention a word, which proves that it was unknown to them. Moreover, Aristotle tells us that if a man knows a thing he can teach it: but the books of the so-called Alchemistic Sages are full of obscurities and a wantonly perplexing phraseology. This shews that their boasted knowledge was an impudent pretence.

Reason Thirteenth.

Many ancient Sages, as well as kings and princes, who had hundreds of profound scholars at their beck and call, have sought the knowledge of this Art in vain; now, this would not have been the case if it had any real existence.

Reason Fourteenth.

Alchemists say that their one Stone changes all metals into gold; this would mean that it hardens lead and tin, which are softer than gold, and that it softens silver, iron, and bronze, which are harder than gold. But it is impossible that one and the same thing should produce opposite effects. If, indeed, it could produce two such mutually exclusive effects, it would have to do the one *per se* and the other *per accidens*—and either that which is hardened or that which is softened would not be true gold. We should thus have to assume the existence of two Stones, one which hardens and colours *per se*, and one which softens and colours *per se;* but this would be in flat contradiction to one of the few clear statements of the Alchemists themselves. And even if there were two different Stones, their difference would be reproduced in their effects, and there would thus result two different kinds of gold, which is impossible.

Reason Fifteenth.

If gold and silver could be evolved out of any metallic substance, they could be prepared most easily out of that which is most closely akin to them; but as it is impossible to prepare them out of their very first principles, viz., quicksilver and sulphur, they cannot be evolved out of metals specifically different from them. For it is clear that out of these two matters all metals are derived and generated; orpiment, sal armoniac, and secondary spirits like marcasite, magnesia, and tutia, being all reducible to these two primary forms. There are seven spirits of Alchemy, the four principal ones, quicksilver, sulphur, orpiment, and sal armoniac, and the three secondary and composite spirits, marcasite, magnesia, and tutia; but sulphur and quicksilver include them all. The Stone would have to be obtained either from the metals or from these spirits. But the Sages represent the Stone as bearing the same relation to the metals which is borne by form to substance, or, soul to body: hence, it cannot be extracted from such gross things as metals. They do indeed say that by calcining, dissolving, distilling, and coagulating those bodies they purge out all that is gross, and render the metals spiritual and subtle. But they know well enough that any fire violent enough to perform this would kill or destroy the vital germ of the metal.

Nor can so highly spiritual a substance as the Philosopher's Stone is represented be obtained from the metallic spirits (sulphur and quicksilver). For they must either be fixed or volatile. If they are volatile they are useless: they evaporate when exposed to the action of fire, and leave bodies still more impure and defiled than they were before; or they even cause other bodies to evaporate along with them. If, on the other hand, the spirits in a fixed state are to represent the Stone, they will not be able to accomplish any of those things which the Stone is supposed to encompass. For, in that case, they are hard and petrine, like earth or flint, and thus are unable to enter other bodies and pervade them with their own essence. If they are subjected to the violent action of fire, they become like glass, *i.e.*, they undergo a process of vitrification, and, with their metallic humour, they lose their malleability and all their other metallic properties. Even lead and tin become glass when their metallic humour is burnt out of them, and it is rank absurdity to say that the vitreous substance is malleable, or ever can become so; for it is the metallic humour which renders metals malleable and fusible. Moreover, glass, or anything vitrified, in melting does not amalgamate with other metals, but floats on the surface like oil. Besides, quicksilver in its natural state adheres to all metals, but it does not adhere either to marcasite (which resembles it too closely for such a purpose), nor to glass: this shews, incontrovertibly, that glass is no metal, whether such glass be natural, or some other substance vitrified. Again, glass, or any vitrified substance, when it has been dipped in cold water, or otherwise refrigerated, can be broken, pounded, and converted into powder; but all metals will bend rather than break, because of their greater malleability and the metallic humour which is in them. You can also either engrave or stamp any image upon cold metals and it will retain that image; but glass (unless in a state of fusion) will do nothing of the kind. Thus, it appears that malleability is a property which belongs to metals, and to metals only; and in the various metals this property, with the property of fusibility, exists in different degrees, according to the grade of their digestion and sulphureous admixtion. In glass, too, there are different proportions of fusibility, perspicuity, opacity, and colouring, which depend upon differences of the material used in its manufacture. Only metals in a cold state are capable of a certain degree of liquefaction; glass, on account of its great viscosity, may be liquefied when it is melted in a fiercely heated furnace, but not after refrigeration, because then the aforesaid viscosity disappears. When metal is cold or red hot its viscosity is greatest, and in such a state it can be expanded; but fusion separates its different parts, and then much of this viscosity is lost. With glass the very opposite is the case. Therefore, if by calcination a metallic spirit becomes vitrified, it is not capable of any further change; and, being fixed, it cannot enter other bodies, or convert them. Therefore, also, if metallic spirits, which are the very vital principles of gold and silver, cannot evolve them out of metals, nothing else can.

Reason Sixteenth.

Again, the Alchemists appear to say that they do not create metals, but only develop those which are imperfect; they call gold and silver perfect metals, and the rest imperfect. We reply that this is an impossibility. The fact is that everything which has its own substantial form, and all its peculiar properties, is specifically perfect. A horse is perfect as a horse, though it has not the rational nature of man; and tin and lead are as perfect in their way as gold and silver. Whatever is perfectly that which it was designed to be, the same also is bound so to remain; thus, lead and tin are fully as permanent and enduring as gold and silver.

Reason Seventeenth.

Again, whatever is multiplied by Nature after its kind, in its own species, may be regarded as permanently belonging to that species And tin and lead, etc., are of this class. They are not an imperfect form of that which we behold perfected in gold and silver. They are base metals, while gold and silver are precious; and a base thing can never develop into a precious thing, just as a goat can never become a horse or a man.

Reason Eighteenth.

Where there is not the same ultimate disposition of elements, there cannot be the same substantial and specific form. Now alchemistic gold and silver cannot exhibit the same ultimate arrangement as natural gold and silver; consequently, they are not the same thing. Hence, if there be such a thing as alchemistic gold, it is specifically different from ordinary gold.

Reason Nineteenth.

Again, those things which have not the same generation, must be, so far, different from each other. Now, gold of Art, if any, is generated by a different process from that which Nature employs. It follows that the gold of Alchemy is not true but fantastical gold.

Reason Twentieth.

Anything that is contingent, and liable to chance, cannot be the subject matter of science: for science deals with the necessary, incorruptible, and eternal. The Alchemists themselves say that the secret of their Art seldom becomes known to any one: hence they themselves put their own claim to scientific accuracy out of court.

Reason Twenty-first.

Again, Aristotle (Meteor. iv.)—according to the ancient version—expressly denies the truth of Alchemy, calling it a sophistical and fantastical pretence—though some say those words were interpolated by Avicenna (which, however, we do not believe). We beg leave to transcribe Aristotle's very words: Let me tell the Alchemists that no true change can take place between species; but they can produce things resembling those they desire to imitate; and they can tinge (*i.e.*, colour) with red and orange so as to produce the appearance of gold, and with white so as to produce the appearance of silver (tin or lead). They can also purge away the impurities of lead (so as to make it appear gold or silver); yet it will never be anything but lead; and even though it look like silver, yet its properties will still be those of lead. So these people are mistaken, like those who take armoniac salt for common salt—which seem the same and yet are in reality very much diverse. But I do not believe that the most exquisite ingenuity can possibly devise any means of successfully eliminating the specific difference (*i.e.*, the substantial form) of metals. The properties and accidents which constitute the specific difference are not such as to be perceived with the senses; and since the difference is not cognizable (*i.e.*, not sensuously perceptible), how can we know whether they have had it removed or not? Moreover, the composition of the various metallic substances is different, and, therefore, it is impossible that one should be changed into another, unless they be first reduced to their common prime substance. But this cannot be brought about by mere liquefaction, though it may appear to be done by the addition of extraneous matter.

By these words the philosopher seems to imply that there can be no such thing as a pure Alchemistic Art, that which passes current under the name being mere fanciful and deceptive talk. From his remarks we elicit five reasons which (apparently) militate against the truth of our Art.

Reason Twenty-second.

[THE FIRST OF ARISTOTLE.]

He who only changes the accidents of things, does not change them specifically, and, as the substantial form remains the same, we cannot say that any real alteration has been effected. Now, the transformation (if any) which takes place in Alchemy is of this kind; therefore, we may confidently assert that it is not real. Alchemists may, as it were, wash out the impurities of lead and tin, and make them look like gold and silver; but in their substantial form they are still neither better nor worse than lead and tin. Certain foreign ingredients (colouring matter, etc.) may make people fancy that they see real gold and silver before them. But those are the same people who could not tell the difference between common salt and salt of ammonia. Nevertheless, these two, though generically the same, exhibit considerable specific differences, and no skilled master of chemistry could possibly confound them.

Reason Twenty-third.
[THE SECOND OF ARISTOTLE.]

Any transformation that does not involve the destruction of the substantial and specific pre-existent form, is no real transformation at all, but a mere juggling pretence. Now this exactly describes the performances of Alchemy.

Reason Twenty-fourth.
[THE THIRD OF ARISTOTLE.]

It is impossible for us to know whether a thing which in itself is incapable of being perceived by our senses has been removed or not. Now, the specific differences of metals belong to this category: therefore, Alchemy falsely claims the power of accomplishing a thing which in reality transcends all human possibility and knowledge. The external characteristics with which we are acquainted in metals are not those which constitute their inward and essential nature, but their accidents, and properties, and passivities, which are alone subject to the cognizance of our senses. If this mysterious and deeply hidden something could be touched and handled, we might hope to destroy, or abolish, and change it. But, as it is, such an attempt must be considered utterly hopeless.

Reason Twenty-fifth.

[THE FOURTH OF ARISTOTLE.]

Things which are not mixed in the same elementary proportions, and are not compounded after the same manner, cannot be regarded as belonging to an identical species. Now, this relation does not exist between natural gold and the metals which Alchemy claims to transmute into that metal. Consequently, they cannot become real gold. The fact is that we are ignorant of the true composition of the precious metals—and how can we bring about a result the nature of which is not clear to us?

Reason Twenty-sixth.

[THE FIFTH OF ARISTOTLE.]

One species can only be transmuted

into another by returning into the first substance common to both, before each was differentiated in the assumption of its own substantial form. This first substance must then be developed into the other species. But such a complicated operation the Alchemists fail to achieve. They do not reduce the metals to the first substance; hence there is with them no true generation, nor is there any genuine corruption, but only a spurious manipulation of accidents. They melt the metal in their furnace, and then add to it certain prepared chemical substances which change its appearance; but no one can say that there has been a true transformation. So long as they do not reduce the metal to its first substance, and then introduce into it another substantial form, it will still be the same metal, whatever alterations they may seem to effect in its outward appearance. The original substance and first principle of gold and silver are quicksilver and sulphur. To this substance they cannot reduce any metal by bare liquefaction. Hence their transmutation of metals is never true, but always sophistical. If you wish to generate a man out of meat and vegetables, and other food that is eaten, this food will first have to become blood, and the blood will have to undergo a chemical change into seed, before it can be available for purposes of generation. In the same way, if any metal is to become gold and silver, it must first become quicksilver and sulphur. The Alchemists may indeed say that there is between metals no specific, but only an accidental difference. They suppose that the base metals are in a diseased condition, while gold and silver exhibit the healthy state of the metallic substance; and thus they contend that lead and tin can be converted into gold and silver by a mere alterative motion, just as an alterative motion (produced by some medicine) may convert a diseased into a healthy man. But this is equivalent to the affirmation that, apart from the morbid matter which they contain, all metals are actually gold, and here is an assertion which it is impossible to substantiate. If all metals have the same substantial form, they have the same properties and passivities; for properties and passivities are directly the outcome of the substantial form. Hence all metals would have the same properties and qualities (whether active or passive) as gold. But this is not the case; for they do not abide the test of fire as gold does, nor have they the same comforting medicinal effect, which proves that the difference between them is not merely accidental, but specific. Yet they might again advance that, though all metals have the same substantial form as gold, they have not the same qualities and properties, because these are kept inactive or obscured by the morbid matter; as, for instance, when a man suffers from epilepsy, or apoplexy, or madness, he cannot perform the operations of a complete man; and if a woman suffer from contraction of the womb, or syncope, she may have the substantial form of a woman, and yet she cannot exercise all the functions of a woman. They further say that, as in the human subject this incapacity is removed by the alterative action of some medicine, so in metals, the full effects of the substantial form (which is that of gold) may be brought out by alchemistic action. But the substantial form is not complete until the development is fully accomplished, and if the base metals are not fully developed, they can have no real substantial form, let alone that of gold and silver. And if a thing have not the same substantial form with anything else, it cannot have, even in a latent condition, the properties and qualities characteristic of that thing. Nothing can have the peculiar qualities of a man that has not the form (*i.e.*, the essential characteristics) of a man. The form of gold consists in the brightness which the sulphur receives from the purifying quicksilver in digestion. This brightness belongs only to gold and silver, or even to gold exclusively, as will be shewn. It is a sign that the development of these precious metals is complete, and the fact that the other metals do not possess it also shews that they cannot have the substantial form or essential characteristics of gold. Hence the comparison of the base metals to diseased bodies is false and misleading. We have thus demonstrated that the claims of Alchemy are frivolous, vain, and impossible. We might adduce other reasons, but we believe those already given to be sufficient.

Now we will proceed to prove the Truth of the Art of Alchemy.

WE may prove the truth of our Art—

(1) By the testimony of the Sages.

(2) By the most forcible arguments.

(3) By analogy, and manifest examples.

(1) Aristotle, in the *Dialectics*, says that every master has a right to speak authoritatively with reference to his own art. According to this rule, it is the Sages, and the Sages only, that ought to be consulted with reference to the truth of Alchemy. Now, we find that ancient philosophers, who have written with remarkable clearness and force on other arts and sciences, have given their testimony to the truth and authenticity of this art in books which they have

devoted thereto. They have described it as an art which regulates natural action, working upon a proper matter, towards the attainment of a design of Nature's own conceiving, to which also Nature cannot attain without the aid of the intelligent artist, the same being further performed, as it is said, after one only method. Hence Hermes: It is true without falsehood, certain, and most true; that which is above is even as that which is below, and that which is below is like unto that which is above, for the accomplishment of the wonders of one thing. And Morienus: If, therefore, thou shalt rightly consider those things which I shall say unto thee, as also the testimonies of the ancients, well and fully shalt thou know that we agree in all things, and do all of us reveal the same truths. This was the deliberate conviction of Hermes, in his *Secreta*, who is styled the father and prophet of the Sages, of Pythagoras, Anaxagoras, Socrates, Plato, Democritus, Aristotle, Zeno, Heraclitus, Diogenes, Lucas,

Hippocrates, Hamec, Thebit, Geber, Rhasis, Haly, Morienus, Theophilus, Parmenides, Mellissus, Empedocles, Abohaly, Abinceni, Homer, Ptolomeus, Virgil, Ovid, and many other philosophers and lovers of truth, whose names it would be tedious to record. Of most of these we have seen and studied the works, and can testify that they were, without a single exception, adepts, and brothers of this most glorious order, and that they knew what they were speaking about. Hermes, in his second book, says: My son, reflect on all that you hear, for I do not suppose that you are deprived of reason, etc. Rhasis (in his book on the *Perfect Magistery*), exhorting us unto a like earnestness, bids us read incessantly the writings of philosophy that we may be her sons, and get understanding in this arcane magistery. For he who does not read books cannot apprehend the details of our Art; he who knows nothing about the theory of our Art, will find its practice very difficult. Geber, in the *Prologue* of his *Sum of*

Perfection, exhorts the student to pore over his volumes by day and by night, and to revolve them diligently in his mind, that so he may perceive the drift of our directions. Galen declares that theory and practice mutually correct and supplement each other. True theory is borne out by practice; false theory is shamed and disgraced by it. Moreover, when the science is obscure, and has been handed down after the manner of a dark tradition, there is all the more reason for reference to the adepts of the past therein. For which reason, says the philosopher in the second book of *Ethics:* In things which are obscure it is necessary to have recourse to open testimonies. So also Morienus: While every thing is distinguished according to its effects, the facts concerning it are more fully confirmed by the testimony of many. Rhasis (c. 70) bids us pin our faith to the ancient sages. Abohaly, that is to say, Avicenna, in his book on *Medicine*, and the chapter in which he discusses the confinement of fevers to certain places, says that where they do not occur, the people would not therefore be justified in supposing that they do not exist. In the same way, no man in his senses would deny the truth of Alchemy for the very insufficient reason that he himself is ignorant of it : such a person would be content with the authority of weighty names like Hermes, Hippocrates, and numerous others. There are many reasons why the masters conceal this art. But if any one denies its existence on the ground that he is ignorant of it, he is like some one who has been shut up all his life in a certain house, and therefore denies that the world extends beyond the four walls of his habitation. There is not really any need to advance any arguments to establish the actuality of our art, for the art itself is the best proof of its own existence ; and being securely lodged in the stronghold of knowledge, we might safely despise the contradiction of the ignorant. Nevertheless, we will adduce a few arguments to prove the strength of our position. At the same time, we ask the reader to remember that our best and strongest arguments are based on facts which we are not at liberty to use.

Arguments [particularly two strong ones] in Favour of our most Glorious Art.

IT is most difficult to establish the claims of this Art argumentatively. Aristotle tells us that, in some cases, certain arguments are so nicely balanced as to leave the mind in a state of uncertainty as to what is the exact truth; in other cases [he says] the subject matter hardly admits of a logical demonstration. To this latter class belongs the case of Alchemy. In all operative sciences (as Aristotle sets forth) the truth of a proposition ought to be shewn, not by logical argument, but by ocular demonstration. The appeal should be not to the intellect, but to the senses. For particulars belong to the domain of sense, while universals belong to the domain of reason. If we are unable to convey to any one an ocular proof of our Art, this fact must not be regarded as casting a slur on our veracity. The difficulty of our task is enhanced by the circumstance that we have to speak of our Art to the ignorant and the scornful, and are thus in the position of a painter who should attempt to explain nice shades and differences of colour to the colour-blind; or of a musician who should discourse sweet harmony to the deaf. Every one, says Aristotle, is able to form a correct opinion only of those things which are familiarly and accurately known to him; but he who denies that snow is white cannot have any eyes in his head. How can any one discover the truth in regard to any science, if he lacks the sense to distinguish the special province of matter, or the material relations, with which that science deals? Such people need to exercise faith even to become aware of the existence of our Art. Pythagoras, in the *Turba Philosophorum*, says that those who are acquainted with the elements will not be numbered among deniers.

A doctor who desires to prove that a certain medicine will produce a certain effect in a diseased condition of the human body, must substantiate his position by practical experiment. For instance, some one suffers from a superabundance of red colour in the veins of the stomach and liver, and I say that the cure is an evacuation after digestion. If I wished to discover what medicine would produce this effect, I would say: Everything that, after digestion, produces an evacuation of bile, will heal the patient. Now, I know that rhubarb or scamonea will produce this effect; therefore, rhubarb or scamonea will be the right remedy to choose. Nevertheless, the truth of my assertion could be satisfactorily proved only by means of a practical experiment. In all these matters, as Hamec says, nothing short of seeing a thing will help you to know it. If you wish to know that pepper is hot and that vinegar is cooling, that colocynth and absinthe are bitter, that honey is sweet, and that aconite is poison; that the magnet attracts steel, that arsenic whitens brass, and that tutia turns it of an orange colour, you will, in every one of those cases, have to verify the assertion by experience. It is the same in Geometry, Astronomy, Music, Perspective, and other sciences with a practical scope and aim. A like rule applies with double force to Alchemy, which undertakes to transmute the base metals into gold and silver. Whatsoever has the power to transmute imperfect and incomplete metals into perfect and complete metals has the power to make gold and silver. Now, this quality is possessed by the Stone which the philosophers make known to us. It is plain that there are but two perfect metals, namely, gold and silver; just as there are but two perfect luminaries, namely, sun and moon. The other metals are imperfect and incomplete, and whosoever educes them to perfection, the same also converts them into gold and silver. The truth and justice of this claim, like all other propositions of a practical nature, has to be demonstrated by a practical experiment, and in no other way can it be satisfactorily shewn. But such a practical demonstration would, on the other hand, once for all put an end to the controversy, and convincingly demonstrate to every well-regulated mind the truth of the Art by which it is accomplished. Find our Art, says Galen, and you will have proved its reality, which is performed not by the first principles of the Art, but by its operations.

It is to be borne in mind that this Art is the minister and follower of Nature. Hence the principles of Alchemy are twofold, natural and artificial. The natural principles are the causes of the four elements, of the metals, and all that belongs to them. The artificial principles are, according to Geber, eight in number: Sublimation, Separation, Distillation, Calcination, Dissolution, Coagulation, Fixion, and Ceration, besides all the tests, signs, and colours by which we know whether these operations have been properly performed or not.

The tests of gold are Incineration, Cementation, Ignition, Fusion, Exposure to corroding vapours, Mixture with some solvent, etc. But there is also another high and divine principle which is the key and connecting link between all the others, without which it is impossible to accomplish our work, which also before all others ought to possess the mind of the student. That which is fixed destroys the specific form of that which is volatile, so as to do away with its volatile properties. If the volatile substance evaporates together with the fixed, the whole experiment is spoiled; but if the fixed retains the volatile and protects it from evaporation, our work is perfected. We know that substances whose root is earth and water can be dissolved and become liquid; in Alchemy their virtues are not destroyed, but the adept has it in his power to preserve them. What is said about this principle in the books of the Sages is without doubt figuratively spoken by means of type and allegory, and therefore it is mere presumption on the part of an outsider to attempt to formulate an argument against our Art out of anything that the Sages have said.

The second argument is as follows. Anything in which the specific properties, qualities, and operations of a certain substance are observed, is of the same nature with that substance. Now, we find in the gold and silver of Alchemy all the distinctive peculiarities of natural gold; consequently, it is natural gold. We do not know the substantial form of anything; we do know its qualities, properties, operations, and accidents; consequently, it is in regard to these particulars that we must look for agreement, because all our knowledge necessarily has a sensuous or perceptive basis. The substantial form, on the other hand, is nothing but a convenient intellectual abstraction. In determining the nature of anything, we must found our judgment on its practical manifestations. We say that whatever performs all the functions of an eye, is an eye; whatever does not is not really an eye, but only the shadow or image of an eye. A wooden saw is not a saw, but only a representation of a saw, etc., etc. I maintain, then, that we know a thing by its accidents; and as the substance of all metals is homogeneous, we may safely apply this rule to metallic substances. Every metal, then, which exhibits all the qualities of gold, orange colour, fusibility, malleability, indestructibility, homogeneous nature, and great density, must be regarded as gold, and it would be mere sophistry to try and make out that it is anything else. If the gold of Alchemy were not the same as natural gold, our detractors would be bound to shew that the very same specific properties can co-exist with substantial forms of an opposite and contradictory nature—a task which they will find it very difficult to accomplish. This reasoning is borne out by several most important passages in the works of Plato and Aristotle [*Libell. de Secret. Secreto, cap. de Lapidibus Pretiosis*]. There are also other arguments which prove the truth of our Art, which will be set forth in our chapters on the principles, and on the generation of metals, and their transmutation.

The Truth of our Art proved by Analogy.

SOMETHING closely analogous to the generation of Alchemy is observed in the animal, vegetable, mineral, and elementary world. Nature generates frogs in the clouds, or by means of putrefaction in dust moistened with rain, by the ultimate disposition of kindred substances. Avicenna tells us that a calf was generated in the clouds, amid thunder, and reached the earth in a stupified condition. The decomposition of a basilisk generates scorpions. In the dead body of a calf are generated bees, wasps in the carcase of an ass, beetles in the flesh of a horse, and locusts in that of a mule. These generations depend on the fortuitous combination of the same elements by which the animal or insect is ordinarily produced. Aristotle (*de Animal.*, 6), however, says, that these creatures do not belong to the same order as those generated in the ordinary way, and have not the same substantial form. We, on the other hand, maintain (and we are sure of having all common-sense people in agreement with us) that ants are ants, flies, flies, and spiders, spiders, in whatever way they originate. For in the vegetable world Nature produces out of decomposed matter, cabbages, parsley, and pumpkins, which afterwards exhibit the same flowers, fruit, and seed as those evolved in the ordinary way, and are also propagated in the same manner. We maintain that there are some things which are propagated by generation only, such as men, vipers, whales, and palm-trees; other things by putrefaction only, as lice, fleas, grass, earthworms, and similar imperfect existences; some things are propagated in both ways, like mice, beetles, wasps, etc. Everything depends, as we have said, on a certain disposition of elements and rearrangement of atoms; in this way a wild vine may become a good one by transplantation and the skill of the husbandman (as Aristotle tells us); moreover, the same philosopher vouches for the truth of the observation that good plants may often be reared from inferior seed, if there be a change of climate and other outward conditions.

The same law holds good in the mineral world, though not to quite so great an extent. Thunderbolts are formed in the clouds, and iron darts, amidst terrible explosions. These mineral substances are produced, according to Aristotle (*Meteor., iv. end*), by the rapid extinction and desiccation of atmospherical fire. It is said that near Vergen there fell from the sky a piece of iron weighing 150 tons, which was so hard that it long resisted all attempts to work it up into swords and other iron implements. The Arabs relate that the Alemanic blades, which are very hard and well tempered, are fashioned of this kind of iron. Such great masses of metal are either formed suddenly by the fierce action of burning heat on a large lump of viscous clay, or, little by little, through the agency of some more gradual cause. There are certain places in which water, as it wells forth, is changed into stones of divers colours; and we know that there exists in the earth the mineral power of congealing water. We are also told that vegetables and animals may be converted into stone by a certain petrifying mineral action. Moreover, there is a spot in Arabia which imbues everything with its own colour. There the bread of Corascenus was changed into a stone, and yet retained its own colour. The same kind of spontaneous generation is also sometimes observed in the case of elements. By striking two hard stones together we produce fire; by boiling water, air is created; by the condensation of air, we obtain water; by the distillation of water, we become possessed of a residue of earth. All these examples we quote, not because they necessarily admit of verification, but in order to make our meaning plain to the uninitiated, and to shew, by analogous reasoning, the possibility of our art. To the initiated such confirmatory evidence, drawn from analogous facts, must seem both childish and unnecessary. Nor is there any process in Nature which is more than distantly and partially analogous to the operation of our most blessed Stone. The closest analogy is furnished by smoke, which may become fixed or condensed as soot; for here a spirit, as it were, evaporates from the fire, and assumes a corporeal form. The same may be said of the formation of tartar in good wine. For all vapour is spiritual in its nature, that is to say, its property is volatile. Out of dry vapours are generated dry things, and from humid vapours come moist substances; the digestion and proportionate commixture of both these kinds produce the diversity of all generated species, according to the exigency of their nature. And as these vapours, whether dry or moist, are actively fugitive and ascending, so are they potentially permanent and resting. If the alchemist by the preparation of this proper matter in a proper vessel, with the suitable degree of fire, paying due attention to the significance of the sequence of colours, can obtain that which constitutes the essence of gold in a concentrated volatile or spiritual form, he can pervade with it every atom of a base metal, and thus transmute it into gold. This action of foreign bodies any one can observe on the surface of metals; tutia imparts to bronze the colour of gold, orpiment and arsenic colour it white like silver; the fumes of Saturn congeal quicksilver; the rind of the pomegranate converts iron into steel, and the fumes of burnt hair give to silver an orange tinge. Let us suppose the metals to be penetrated by some more powerful and all-pervading agent in their very inmost parts, and throughout all their molecules, — and we have something very closely resembling the alleged action of the Philosopher's Stone. The spirits of metals potentially contain their bodies, and this potentiality may at any moment become actual, if the artist understands, and knows how to imitate, Nature's methods of working.

A General Determination upon the Difficulty of the Question, with the Elucidation thereof.

CONCERNING this admirable, excellent, divine, and most secret Art, it is a matter of no ordinary difficulty to satisfactorily resolve the question of the actuality thereof, but, as appears from Aristotle, it is absurd to prove the existence of Nature, or to argue the possibility of what is known. Our subject is the transmutation of metals into true gold and silver by the skill of art. It deals not alone with the formation of metals in the earth but of their manufacture out of the earth. Alchemy is the Art by which the principles, causes, activities, properties, and affections of metals are thoroughly apprehended; and by means of this knowledge those metals which are imperfect, incomplete, mixed, and corrupt, and therefore base, are transmuted into gold and silver. We have here, as in medicine, practice founded upon sound and well-tested speculative knowledge; and here also, as in medicine, we can be practically successful, only if our knowledge be strictly in accordance with the facts of Nature. Alchemy is an operative science, and produces effects by supplying natural conditions, *e.g.*, by the action of fire. Medicine is either preventive or curative; it either teaches us the conditions of health, and instructs us how to avoid disease, or, when we are ill, it provides the exact remedy which our disease requires. Alchemy has no need of conservative or preventive action; but it instructs us how to restore and cure, as it were, the diseases of metals, and to bring them back to a state of perfect health, in which state all metals are either silver or gold. The difficulties of our Art are great, especially on account of the disagreement which apparently prevails amongst its most authoritative exponents. The second difficulty of our

Art is that of carrying out practically the clearest and most straightforward printed directions. This difficulty might be got over by watching the operations of some great master; but in the nature of the case, only few can enjoy so high a privilege. The third difficulty consists in the fantastic tricks and absurdly barren devices of fraudulent professors of this Art, in consequence of which many find it impossible to believe in the reality of our operations. And the claims of the Art itself appear so miraculous, and so far exalted above the ordinary course of Nature, that the vulgar herd are of necessity led to regard the Alchemist as a kind of sorcerer or magician, and to place his pretensions in the same class with those of the man who professes to work signs and wonders. These are but a few of the difficulties in which the study of our Art is involved; and if there be so many obstacles in the way of its investigation, how much more difficult must be the discovery of its methods?

Nevertheless, I stoutly maintain that the Art of Alchemy is clear and true, and founded upon Nature; that its products are as truly silver and gold as the precious metals which are produced in the bowels of the earth; and that I am fully prepared to substantiate all these assertions in the following chapters, and to place them beyond the reach of reasonable doubt. We will triumphantly rebut the attacks of Aristotle, and refute all other objections, putting them to flight with the all-prevailing weapons of truth and reason. Aristotle, in *Nicom. Ethic.* vii., says that if all difficulties are solved, and the contrary of every objection proved to be true, you can feel that you have established your position, but your refutation will be all the more convincing if you point out the cause of your opponent's error. If, however, any man denies first principles, there is no possibility of reasoning with him; on the other hand, you can reason with a man who acknowledges first principles, and only arrives at erroneous results by a fallacious process of ratiocination. It is to this class of our opponents that we address the following statement of our position.

Explanatory of our Method of Procedure in Determining this Question.

BUT in order that the truth of this Art may be fully known, we will begin by citing the authority, and quoting the words of, the ancient Sages, subsequently resolving any doubt or difficulty which they may suggest. In every case we will take care to state our reasons. Any one that would write about Alchemy must know its terms, with its differences and its scope ; and it is their ignorance of these particulars which has led many critics hastily to condemn our claims. Those who are ignorant of any science, are like the spectators who can distinguish neither the persons nor their gestures on the stage. A blind man might as well discourse about colours, and criticize the merits of a picture — a deaf man might as well set up as a judge of some musical composition—as an uninformed person presume to deliver judgment on the claims of the Art of Alchemy.

The scope and aim of that Art we have already defined. It is an operative science, of which the object is to transmute base metals into gold and silver. It is concerned with the principles, causes, properties, and affections of metals. Principles are the efficient and final cause, which are both outward. Causes are described as the substance and form, which are the internal causes belonging to the very thing itself. Properties are the peculiar active operations of the metals (*e.g.*, the strengthening virtue of gold). Affections are the qualities of metals in a passive state, *e.g.*, the power of gold to resist the operation of fire, and so on. The essential differences between the metals we do not know: hence we allege in their place the properties and accidents peculiar to each. It should further be remembered that no natural agent ceases from its action in a given substance until its end has been attained. In all metals quicksilver is understood for the substance, and sulphur for the active principle which supplies form to the matter; no metal is, therefore, complete and perfect, from which the sulphur has not become separated; and since this is the case only in gold, gold alone can properly be called a perfect metal—gold alone represents the first and true intention of Nature with regard to metals; all other metals still contain an admixture of sulphur, and are imperfect. The incomplete metals are called mixed metals, because here the agent is still mixed with the substance; and this sulphur is one of the great occasions of the corruptibility of metals: it blackens them, and causes them to evaporate and be burned in the fire, but gold ever enjoys immunity from this defect, whether in or out of the fire. The transmutation of metals into gold, then, must consist in the elimination of this sulphur, which result is brought about only by the Philosopher's Stone, and by that instantly, for it acts both within and without, the exterior alterations being followed by the interior transmutation for the generation of the form of gold. Alchemy (*i.e.*, the Elixir of Alchemy) is a corporeal substance, made of one thing, by the operation of one thing, says Lilium. In medicine we apply the same name both to the science and to the remedy which it prescribes; and a like analogy we must be permitted to follow in our most glorious Art of Alchemy.

AFTER SHEWING THE TWO
CHIEF DIFFICULTIES OF ALCHEMY,
WE PROCEED TO EXHIBIT ALL
THE DIFFERENT MODES OF
THESE DIFFICULTIES.

TO one who is acquainted with the scope and meaning of this Art, it is not so strange that only few attain to our knowledge; to him the wonder is rather that any man has ever succeeded in discovering its methods.

The First Cause of Difficulty.

The achievements of our Art seem miraculous rather than in accordance with the ordinary working of Nature. Hence Sages like Hermes, Barsenus, Rhasis, Rosinus, and others, tell us that it is only by Divine inspiration, or by ocular demonstration, that the student can understand the directions of his teachers. Morienus warns us that whoever would study this Art must know the other sciences, and especially Logic and Dialectic, as the Sages always express themselves in veiled and metaphorical phraseology. Theophilus says that the only way of apprehending the meaning of the Sages is by constant reference to experiment as well as reading [*Turba*]. He who bends his back over our books (says Barsenus), and does not sit at the feet of Nature, will die on the wrong side of the frontier. The first great difficulty, then, is the obscurity of the directions found in the books of the Sages.

Second Cause of Difficulty.

The second difficulty consists in the apparent disagreement of those who profess to exercise our Art at the present day. Amongst these persons are observed a great diversity of method, and a considerable variety even in the choice of their substance. The mistakes of some of the professors of Alchemy make men doubt the genuineness of its claims.

Third Cause of Difficulty.

Again, there are very few that actually possess the Stone. The pretensions of those who boast that it is in their possession discredit the Art in the eyes of the multitude.

Fourth Cause of Difficulty.

The expressions used by the different Masters often appear to be in open contradiction one to another; moreover, they are so obscurely worded that of ten readers each one would understand them in a different sense. Only the most ingenious and clearsighted men have a chance of finding their way through this pathless thicket of contradictions and obscure metaphors.

Fifth Cause of Difficulty.

Another difficulty is the way in which the substance of our Stone is spoken of by the Sages. They call it the vilest and commonest of all things, which is found among the refuse in the street and on the dunghill; yet they add that it cannot be obtained without considerable expense. They seem to say in the same breath that it is the vilest and that it is the most precious of all substances. One man affirms that it is so costly that much gold will not buy it; and, on the other hand, Daucus tells us that we are to beware of foolishly spending gold in the pursuit of this Magistery.

Moreover, from what has been said, we can see that all the names of this Stone are fictitious and misleading. This indeed is the constant practice of the Sages, as Rosinus adds, though he makes an exception of Hermes, who says: Know that no true Tincture is obtained except from the Red Stone. But most of the directions which we find in the books of the Sages cause us to mix the true substance with many foreign ingredients, and thus to mar our work. How, then, shall we, by considering their works only superficially, and according to their literal interpretation, fathom the profound knowledge required for the practical operations of this Magistery? If the base metals are to attain the fixed nature of gold, says Rhasis, we shall need much labour, much meditation, much patient study, and constant reference of the words of the Sages to the facts of Nature, which alone can explain them.

Sixth Cause of Difficulty.

The tropical expressions and equivocations, the allegories, and metaphors, employed by the Sages, also create a most serious obstacle in the path of the student. Hence investigation, and the practical operations which should be based upon it, are embarrassed at every step with doubt and perplexity of the most tantalising kind. We must not wonder, therefore, that the students and professors of Alchemy are peculiarly liable to error, since it is often all but impossible to do more than guess at the meaning of the Sages. At times it would almost look as if this Art could be acquired only by the living voice of the Master, or by direct Divine inspiration.

Seventh Cause of Difficulty.

Every other science and art is closely reasoned; the different propositions follow each other in their logical order; and each assertion is explained and demonstrated by what has gone before. But in the books of our Sages the only method which prevails is that of chaos; there is everywhere studied obscurity of expression; and all the writers seem to begin, not with first principles, but with that which is quite strange and unknown to the student. The consequence is that one seems to flounder along through these works, with only here and there a glimmering of light, which vanishes as soon as one approaches it more closely. Such is the opinion of Rosinus, Anaxagoras, and other Sages.

Eighth Cause of Difficulty.

The way in which the Sages speak of the vessel in which the decoction is to take place, is very perplexing. They give directions for preparing and using many different kinds of vessels, and yet in the same breath they tell us, after the manner of Lilium, that only one vessel is needed for the entire process of decoction! It is true that the words of the Sages about the one invariable vessel become plain as soon as we understand the Art, but to the beginner they must appear very perplexing.

Ninth Cause of Difficulty.

The proper duration of our Magistery, and the day and hour of its nativity and generation, are also shrouded in obscurity. Its conception, indeed, takes place at one single moment; here we are to notice the conjunction of the purified elements and the germ of the whole matter; but if we do not know this, we know nothing of the entire Magistery. There are certain signs which occur with great regularity, at their own proper times and seasons, in the development of this Stone; but if we do not understand what they are, we are as hopelessly in the dark as before. The same remark applies to the exact proportions in which the different elements enter into its composition. The time required for the whole work is stated by Rhasis to be one year; Rosinus fixes it at nine months; others at seven; others at forty, and yet others at eighty, days. Still we know that as the hatching of a chicken is always accomplished in the same period, so a certain number of days or months, and no more, must be required for this work. The difficulty connected with the time also involves the secret of the fire, which is the greatest mystery of the Art. The day when the Stone will be finished may be predicted from certain signs, if they are only known to us, just as the day when an infant will be born may be predicted from the time when it first begins to move in its mother's womb. These critical periods, however, are nowhere clearly and straightforwardly declared to us; and there is all the more need of care, vigilance. and attention on our part.

Tenth Cause of Difficulty.

The Sages appear to vary quite as much in their descriptions of the substance from which this Stone is elaborated. In order to mislead the ignorant and the foolish, some name arsenic, some sulphur, some quicksilver, some blood, some eggs, some hair, some dung, etc., etc. In reality, there is only one substance of our Stone; nothing else upon earth contains it; it is that which is most like gold, and from which gold itself is generated, viz., pure quicksilver, that is, not mixed with anything else, as we shall shew further on. The substance of Alchemy—though called by a perplexing variety of names—is the substance of Nature, and the first substance of metals, from which Nature herself evolves them. Were it otherwise, it would be impossible for Art to imitate Nature.

Aristotle says that the more unity and simplicity of subject-matter and method there are in an art, the more easily is it known; and when we once possess the necessary preliminary knowledge, his words apply with remarkable force to our Art. That Art would be mere child's play, if the Sages had expounded it as simply and plainly as they might have done. But let us tell ignorant professors of Alchemy that the more complicated and sophisticated their methods, the more hopelessly are they at variance with the simple and all-prevailing truth of Nature.

OUR ART IS SHEWN TO BE ONE, NOT ONLY IN ITS SUBSTANCE, BUT IN ALL OTHER RESPECTS. THE UNITY OF THE PHILOSOPHER'S STONE IS MAINTAINED IN ITS SUBSTANCE, AND IN ITS METHOD OF OPERATION, WHICH ADMITS OF NO FOREIGN ELEMENTS.

THE substance of our Art is one, and admits of no variation or substitute, and so also the mode of our Art is one. The unity of our Art is proved by the fact that, though the Sages exhibit considerable diversity in their methods of expressing themselves, yet they all understand each other. The very fact that Greek understands Greek, and Latin Latin, and Arab Arab, proves the unity of each language; and it is the same with our Art. Amidst the greatest apparent diversity there is a wonderful substantial agreement in the works of the Sages; they differ in words, names, and metaphors, but they agree in reference to things. By one way, says Lilium, by one thing, by one disposition is our whole Magistery accomplished. So Alphidius tells us that we want only one thing, viz., water, etc. With these sayings agree the words of Mahometh, Morienus, Geber, Rhasis, Solomon, the son of David, Senior, and Mundus, in the *Turba*, who says: Nature delights in the same nature, kind in kind, kind overcomes kind, kind contains kind, and yet they are not different kinds, or several, but only one kind, having within itself those properties by which it excels all other things. So Haly remarks in his *Mysteries*: Know, brother, that our whole Magistery is one Stone, which is self-sufficient, is not mixed with anything else, proceeds from one root, becomes several things, and yet again is restored to its unity. This one thing is described by the Sages in many ways, and thus it has been supposed to be many things. But such mistaken impressions are characteristic of those who profess our Art without really knowing anything about it.

Instances against the said Unity.

It appears indeed as if there were many roads to our Art, and not one only. Geber avers that there are many ways to produce one effect. The same opinion is expressed by Rhasis in his book on the *Perfect Magistery*, where he speaks of bodies and spirits, and their purification and divers and manifold composition. We answer, as before, that there is only one way and one substance, as shall be abundantly demonstrated hereafter. The words of Rhasis are indeed true, but in our substance body and spirit are the same thing in different stages of development. And so, whether body or spirit, that which is perfectly prepared, the same is the pure and one Elixir. It is in like manner with regard to plurality of methods: food nourishes, but the stages by which this result is brought about are many, as every physiologist will tell you. If there seem to be many methods, they are all only aspects and subdivisions of our *one* method. The White Stone and the Red Stone, the medicine of the third order, as Geber tells us it should be called, are really the same thing; the White Stone is only less perfect than the Red. Nature, says Florus, is one, and if any man strays away from her guidance, he mars his labour. You do not require many things, but only one thing which has a father and mother, and its father and mother feed and nourish it, nor can it be distinguished in any way from its father and mother. From the one substance is evolved, first the White, and then the Red Tincture; there is one vessel, one goal, and one method. It is true that in the books of the Sages the impression is conveyed as if there were many substances and many methods: but they only mean different aspects or stages of the same thing. Solution, Sublimation, Distillation, Coagulation, Calcination, etc., are misleading terms; the distinctions are logical, or verbal, rather than real. Pythagoras tells us that Coction, Calefaction, Dealbation, Attrition, Affusion, and Tinging are only different stages of the same operation in the fire. There are many names, but one regimen.

THE FIRST DISTINCTION SHEWETH THAT THIS ART IS NATURAL AND DIVINE, AND THAT BY IT THE ANCIENT SAGES FORETOLD THE FUTURE MIRACLES OF GOD.

Our Art is partly natural and partly supernatural, or Divine. In changing the base metals into gold and silver by the projection of the Stone, it follows (by an accelerated process) the method of Nature, and therefore is natural. But if we consider the digestion and generation, the conception and origin, of the Stone, we have, in Sublimation, the creation of a soul through the mediation of the spirit, and rising heavenward with the spirit. At another stage we have the soul and spirit permanently fixed at the end of the Sublimation; and this happens through the addition of the Hidden Stone, which is not sensuously apprehended, but only known intellectually, by revelation or inspiration. Alexander says: There are two stages in this Art, that which you see with the eye, and that which you apprehend with the mind. The hidden Stone may be called the gift of God, and if it does not mingle with our Stone, the work of Alchemy is marred. Now, the same hidden Stone is the heart and tincture of gold sought by the Sages. In this way, Alchemy is supernatural and Divine, and in this Stone consists the whole difficulty of the Art. We have need of faith in this matter, just as much as we have need of it in regard to God's miraculous dealings in Scripture. It is God alone that perfects our Stone, and Nature has no hand in it. It is on account of this fact that the ancient Sages were able to prophecy: the influence of the supernatural Stone exalted them above the ordinary level of human nature. The prophecies which they uttered were frequently of a special and most important character. Though heathens, they knew that there would come for this world a day of judgment and consummation; and of the resurrection of the dead, when every soul shall be reunited to its body, not to be severed from it thenceforward for ever. Then they said that every glorified body would be incorruptible, and perfectly penetrated in all its parts by the spirit, because the nature of the body would then resemble that of the spirit. Bonellus, in the *Turba* says: All things live and die at the beck of God, and there is a nature which on becoming moist, and being mingled with moisture for some nights, resembles a dead thing; thereafter it needs fire, till the spirit of that body is extracted, and the body becomes dust. Then God restores to it its soul and spirit. Its weakness is removed, and it is raised incorruptible and glorious. Our substance conceives by itself, and is impregnated by itself, and brings forth itself—and this, the conception of a virgin, is possible only by Divine grace. Moreover, the birth leaves our substance still a virgin, which, again, is a miraculous event. Hence we cannot but call the conception, birth, and nutrition of our Stone supernatural and divine. Alphidius tells us that our Stone is cast out into the streets, raised aloft to the clouds, dwells in the air, is nourished in the river, sleeps upon the summits of mountains; its mother is a virgin, its father knows no woman. These ancient Sages also knew that God must become man, because on the last day of our Magistery that which generates, and that which is generated, become absolutely one; then the old man and the child, and the father and the son, are indistinguishably united. Hence they concluded that the Creator must also become one with the creature; moreover, they knew that man was, alone of all created beings, made in the image of God. Plato wrote the Gospel, which many years later was re-written and completed by S. John, even as S. Augustine recites in the eighth book of his *Confessions*. Our Magistery, says Morienus, is the Mystery of Mysteries of the Most High God, which He committed to His saints in Paradise.

It is to be noted that natural operations which lie out of the course of ordinary natural development, have in them a Divine or supernatural element. And the power which is in Nature is also derived from God. Our Magistery depends quite as much on Divine influences as upon the operations of Nature, and the succour of the artist who assists Nature. The change is brought about by the power of God, which operates through the knowledge of the artist. How difficult, how mysterious, how wonderful, how arduous must it then be for the artist to attain to so lofty a summit of spiritual insight! We may well call this Magistery a divine and glorious mystery, which transcends not only Nature, but the godlike reason of man;

for even man cannot apprehend the mystery, except by direct inspiration or by circumstantial oral teaching, combined with minute ocular demonstration.

HERE FOLLOWS THE SECOND DISTINCTION, IN WHICH SHALL BE SHEWN HOW THIS ART WAS INVENTED; TO WHOM IT IS GIVEN, FROM WHOM IT IS WITHHELD, AND WHY THE SAGES KEEP IT SUCH A CLOSE SECRET.

None of the ancients would have been able to bring to light the hidden mysteries of this Art, had not God Himself, the Bestower of all good and perfect gifts, first revealed it to His Saints that feared His Holy Name. Rhasis, in his *Book of Three Words*, calls it the gift of God. Aristotle says that it was first known to Adam. Others affirm that it was revealed to Enoch in a vision; and these persons identify Enoch with Hermogenes, or Hermes Trismegistus. Aristotle, in his *Epistle to Alexander*, calls the origin of the Art one of the greatest and most sacred mysteries; and therefore he entreats that prince not to ask for more information than he gives him in the said treatise. Some persons indeed maintain that this treatise is a rank forgery, and that it was certainly not composed by Aristotle; and this opinion they base on internal evidence, more especially on the difference in style which may be observed in the book when compared with the other writings of the illustrious Stagirite. But the diffence of style is sufficiently accounted for by the exceptional nature of the subject matter: and this epistle has always been attributed to Aristotle. Testimony is borne to the same fact also by John Mesve, and in Haly's book on the *Mystery of Mysteries*. Now because this Art was revealed by God to His obedient servants, it is the duty of all Sages not to reveal it to any unworthy person. It is true that whoever understands a science, or art, knows how to teach it; nor would jealousy or envy become a wise man: but the Sages have expressed their knowledge in mysterious terms in order that it might be made known to no person except such as were chosen by God Himself. But though the phraseology of the Sages be obscure, it must not therefore be supposed that their books contain a single deliberate falsehood. There are many passages in the writings of Morienus, Geber, and others, where this charge is indignantly rebutted. Those for whom the knowledge of Alchemy is intended, will be able, in course of time and study, to understand even the most obscure of Alchemistic treatises: for they will be in a position to look at them from the right point of view. It is only the wise and God-fearing whom we invite to this banquet: let those who are not bidden refrain from attempting to cross our threshold. The books of our Sages are only for the Sons of Knowledge. The Sages, says Hermes, are not jealous of the obedient, gentle, and lowly student: it is the profane, the vicious, and the ignorant to whom they desire to give a wide berth.

Therefore, I conjure you, my friends, not to make known this science to any foolish, ignorant, or unworthy person. God-fearing Sages, adds Alphidius, have never carried their jealousy so far as to refuse to unveil this mystery to men of their own way of thinking. But they have carefully concealed it from the multitude, lest there should be an end of all sowing, planting, reaping, and of agriculture and work generally. These are very good and humane reasons, then, why this Art should not be revealed to everybody. Moreover, it is delivered to us in obscure terms, in order that the student may be compelled to work hard in its pursuit. We do not prize that which costs us nothing; it is our highest delight to reap some great benefit as the reward of our labour. Therefore, it would not be good for you if this knowledge were to come to you after reading one book, or after spending a few days in its investigation. But if you are worthy, if you possess energy and the spirit of perseverance, if you are ready to study diligently by day and by night, if you place yourself under the guidance of God, you will find the coveted knowledge in God's own good time. Do not be satisfied with alteration of metals, like our modern sophists, but aim at transmutation; and do not suffer them to lead you aside with their sophistical jargon and their absurd and baseless pretensions. Knowledge is one, as truth is one; and let me add that our knowledge and our truth are both very simple and straightforward. If you once depart from the unity and truth of Nature, you are involved in the bewildering mazes of confusion and error.

OBSERVE HERE THE OPERATION AND EXPERIENCE OF ALCHEMY, HOW IT CALLS FOR CONSTANT MANUAL OPERATIONS, AND THE TEACHING OF EXPERIENCE, FOR THE ARTIST TO PURIFY THE ELEMENTS, AND TO COMBINE THEM WHEN PURIFIED, ETC.

In our glorious Art nothing is more necessary than constant reference to the facts of Nature, which can be ascertained only by actual experiment. The dross which is purged off by means of the natural operation must be removed by the artist, if his work is to prosper. The philosopher Socrates directs us to seek the cold of the Moon that we may find the heat of the Sun, and to exercise the hands so that the laborious nature of the work may be lightened. Hence it is all but impossible, as we may learn from Geber in his *Sum of Perfection*, for a blind man, or one whose sense of touch is defective, or for a man without hands, to be successful in our Magistery. The experience of sight is essential, more especially at the end of the decoction; when all superfluous matter has been removed, the artist will behold an awful and amazing splendour, the occultation of Sol in Luna, the marriage of East and West, the union of heaven and earth, and the conjunction, as the ancients tell us, of the spiritual with the corporeal. In that process of cooling, as we may learn from the *Turba Phil-*

osophorum, Hermes, and Avicenna, the manifest is concealed, while that which was concealed is made manifest. The first operation, which is done by hand, is the first stage of the work, which consists in Sublimation and Purification. The second operation, in which the artist has nothing to do but to look on, is the second stage of the work. Here the purified and sublimed substance is fixed and becomes solid. This operation should bring about the perfection of our substance. No one can exercise our Magistery in the absence of the practical teaching of experience, without which the most diligent poring over books would be useless. The words of the Sages may mean anything or nothing to one who is not acquainted with the facts which they describe. If the son of knowledge will persevere in the practical study of our Art, it will in due time burst upon his enchanted vision. The study of books cannot be dispensed with, but the study of books alone is not sufficient. There must be a profound natural faculty for interpreting the significance of those symbols and analogies of the philosophers, which in one place have one meaning and in another a different. For, as Morien tells us, all books on Alchemy are figuratively written. By theory and practice working together, you will be led to the fruition of the most precious arcanum, which is the greatest and most wonderful treasure of this world. If you think that you have understood the directions of the Sages, put your impression to a practical test; if you were mistaken, Nature will take good care to correct your error, and if you will follow her guidance and take her suggestions, she may, after several experiments, put you in the right path. Thus you must go on, letting theory suggest practice, and correcting practice by theory, until at length all difficulties are resolved, and your way lies plain before you. Meditation, says Rhasis, is of no value without experience, but it is possible for you to gain your object by experience without meditation. The practical method will at once enable you to detect any false or sophistical statement, and to avoid being infected with the folly of our modern Alchemists. You will never, for instance, fall into so gross a mistake as to suppose that our Art can change common flints into diamonds or other precious stones. Those who put forward such a statement do not seem to understand that there is here wanting that identity of first substance which undoubtedly exists in the case of base and precious metals. The products of such an art (falsely so called) are not diamonds or precious stones, but pieces of glass, the colouring matter of which is supplied from without, and not—as it ought to be—from within. Moreover, even if we really knew the precise nature of the first substance of precious stones, we could hardly produce them, because they are not fusible like metals. Against all such errors the practical Alchemist will be on his guard. It is impossible for us to imitate Nature in the production of substances of which we have only the proximate matter, and are in ignorance of the mode of their acting, as, for example, in marcasite, tutia, and antimony, of which the matter is quicksilver and sulphur; much less then can we imitate her in the manufacture of precious stones when we are ignorant in both points.*

Third Distinction, shewing that this Art is more certain than other Sciences, and that it is Noble, Brief, and very Easy.

The remarkable agreement of all Sages demonstrates that this Art is more certain than any other. There is amongst them a wonderful speculative and practical harmony, and their contradictions are only verbal and superficial. The whole Magistery of our Art can be learned in a single hour of one who knows—which is the case with no

---

* Bonus was a contemporary of Raymond Lully, and was therefore unacquainted with his treatise on the composition of precious stones.

other science or Art. Yet one who can perform the practical operations of Alchemy is not yet an Alchemist, just as not every one who speaks grammatically is a grammarian. Such persons still lack that knowledge of the causes of things which exalts the mind of man, and raises it to God. Hermes, in the beginning of his *Book of Mysteries*, calls Alchemy a most true and certain Art, shewing that what is above is like that which is beneath, and that which is beneath is like that which is above, etc., etc. Again, our Art is more noble and precious than any other science, Art, or system, with the single exception of the glorious doctrine of Redemption through our Saviour Jesus Christ. It must be studied, not, like other Arts, for gain, but for its own sake; because itself has power to bestow gold and silver, and knowledge more precious than either gold or silver. It may also be called noble, because there is in it a Divine and supernatural element. It is the key of all good things, the Art of Arts, the science of sciences. There are, according to Aristotle, four noble sciences: Astrology, Physics, Magic, and Alchemy—but Alchemy bears the palm from them all. Moreover, it is a science which leads to still more glorious knowledge; nor can there be found a branch of human wisdom, either speculative or practical, to equal it. We naturally desire, says Aristotle *(de Animal.,* 10*)*, to know a little of a noble and profound science, rather than to understand thoroughly some commonplace branch of knowledge. Our Art frees not only the body, but also the soul from the snares of servitude and bondage; it ennobles the rich, and comforts and relieves the poor. Indeed, it may be said to supply every human want, and to provide a remedy for every form of suffering.

It has been set forth by the Sages in the most perplexing and misleading manner, in order to baffle foolish and idly curious persons, who look rather at the sound than at the meaning of what is said. Yet, in spite of foolish and ignorant people, the Art is one, and it is true. Were it stripped of all figures and parables, it would be possible to compress it into the space of eight or twelve lines.

This Art is noble, brief, and easy. It requires one thing, which everybody knows. It is in many things, yet it is one thing. It is found everywhere, yet it is most precious. You must fix it and tame it in the fire; you must make it rise, and again descend. When conjunction has taken place, straightway it is fixed. Then it gives riches to the poor and rest to the weary. The operation is good, if it become first dry and then liquid, and what Rebis (Twothing) is, you will find in the practical part of this work.

Fourth Distinction, shewing the Error into which many fall towards the end of the Work, namely, in the Composition of Elements; what is the Beginning of the Work and what is its End; and how this Art is not for all wise people.

It is difficult enough to know and investigate natural things, and their causes; but the knowledge of supernatural things is proportionately still more difficult. Hence we must not be surprised that the mysteries of our Art are discovered only by few enquirers. It is not good fortune, but only the grace of God, joined to reason, that will ensure success.

Many students of our Art who have operated naturally only, have accomplished the first part of our Magistery; but as the second part contains a supernatural element, being ignorant and incredulous, they were not able to perform it, and thus that which they had already done was neither permanent nor valuable. For there can be no permanence in the first part unless it be joined to the second in the same hour, for the second is the key of the whole work. I knew a man, says Gregory, who began the work in the right way, and achieved the white Tincture; but when there was some delay about the appearance of the Red Colour, he gave up in despair, etc. This man knew the simple elements of our Art, their purification, commixtion, and the different signs which were to appear; he was ignorant only of the day and hour in which the conjunction of the simple elements and the completion of the work might be expected; and because he did not know what to do at that time, the whole Magistery vanished from his sight. For the White Stone was not yet fixed, and, being exposed to too much heat, it evaporated. The permanent fixation of the Stone is the Divine or supernatural department in our Art, which is performed by the composition of these simple elements together, when the fixed Stone retains the volatile, and they remain together eternally, wherein is the whole power of Alchemy, which is neither accomplished by Art or Nature only, but by God the glorious. I do you to wit, says Lucas in *The Crowd*, that all things created are composed of four elements, and return into them; in these they are generated and corrupted, according to the will of God. It is through the shortcomings of their creation, as Alphidius testifies, that all things are subject to decay. Our Stone must have the elements so cunningly united in its composition that they can never thenceforward be separated. You need special pains towards the end of our Magistery. The fœtus grows without any care, day by day and hour by hour, for nine months in the mother's womb; but when its growth is completed, it needs an expulsive effort of the uterus, or else it must die; and something of the same kind happens with regard to our Stone, which, though it is produced perfect in itself, is yet wanting in tincture fixity, and marital conjunction. When the hatching of chickens is accomplished, the little creatures often want some aid to assist them in getting out of the egg, and if they cannot obtain that aid they are choked and die. We must know, says Rhasis, the hidden nature of the Stone and of its dissolution; for if you have not an accurate knowledge of these particulars you had better stay your hand at once. Let us not for a moment suppose that it will be profitable for us to set about this Magistery if we do not understand the composition of the elements. This is the part of our work which is supernatural, since it unites earthly to heavenly things, and therefore it is called Divine, celestial, glorious, wonderful, most beautiful, most difficult. It is an Art which we can know by Divine inspiration. The ancient Sages described the entire first part of the work as the beginning of the work, and the beginning of the work was with them the nativity and germination of the Stone, which takes place on the day when the coction and digestion of the substance is complete, and its sublimation perfect. In other words, to them the beginning of the work was the completion of the digestive process, and the digested and perfected substance itself. The end and complement of the work is the retaining of the Stone after its digestion. Now, Aristotle tells us that a slight error in the beginning may be a great one in the end; one mistake breeds a whole swarm of disastrous consequences. Hence we must be very careful about the first steps we take in the development of our substance, or we may irreparably mar our work at the very outset, the error becoming more and more apparent as the operation proceeds. The perfection of the end must be already germinally contained in the beginning. Whiteness is the beginning of our Magistery, its perfection and end is Redness; and the Red Tincture is germinally contained in the white. The spirit cannot enter the body until it is purified; but when purification has taken place, we may expect the permanent conjunction of the corporeal and the spiritual principles. So should the state of whiteness be anxiously looked for, because it is the beginning and foundation of this work.

HERE FOLLOWS THE FIFTH DISTINCTION, SHEWING THAT THIS STONE IS LIKE ALL THINGS IN THE WORLD, AND THAT IT GOES BY DIFFERENT NAMES. HOW FAR ALCHEMY HAS ANYTHING IN COMMON WITH OTHER SCIENCES.

Our Stone, from its all-compehensive nature, may be compared to all things in the world. In its origin and sublimation, and in the conjunction of its elements, there are analogies to things heavenly, earthly, and infernal, to the corporeal and the incorporeal, to things corruptible and incorruptible, visible and invisible, to spirit, soul, and body, and their union and separation, to the creation of the world, its elements, and their qualities, to all animals, vegetables, and minerals, to generation and corruption, to life and death, to virtues and vices, to unity and multitude, to actuality and potentiality, to conception and birth, to male and female, to boy and old man, to the vigorous and the weak, to the victor and the vanquished, to peace and war, to white and red, and all colours, to the beauty of Paradise, to the terrors of the infernal abyss.

To the initiated it is clear that Moses, Daniel, Solomon, several of the prophets, and the evangelist S. John, possessed the knowledge of this Art, it having been revealed to them by God Himself. These holy men did not affect the Art for the sake of the acquisition of gold and silver, but on account of its beauty and the insight which it affords into the things of the spiritual world. As our Art is touched upon in all other sciences, so the prophets referred to it for the purpose of illustrating Divine truth. Nor is this wonderful, seeing that our Art speaks of all things, both visible and invisible, by analogy. This remark refers not only to philosophy, physics, medicine, astrology, geomancy, etc., but is of universal application.

It may be asserted as a general truth that the verities and realities of things come first, while their similitudes and allegories are secondary and derivative. The ancient Sages, before Aristotle, were therefore greatly mistaken in supposing that any art or science could be taught or delivered to others by means of allegories and metaphorical analogies. Before an Art is known, it should be taught—according to Aristotle, Averroes, and Avicenna—by a plain and straightforward method; when it is once known, the allegorical method may be employed with advantage.

Owing to the custom of the Sages, that, namely, of giving an allegorical expression to their meaning, and carefully eschewing the plain scientific method, we have an infinite variety of names used to describe our precious

Stone, every one of which may be said, in a tropical manner, to represent a certain aspect of the truth of our Art. So Rhasis in the *Light of Lights* warns us that his sayings are to be typically understood. The same principle may open up to us an understanding of the paradoxical assertion of Pythagoras—in *The Crowd*—that our Stone is found everywhere and yet not found; it is a stone and not a stone, worthless and precious, carefully hidden and yet familiarly known to all, with one name and yet many names. The great variety of its names is referred by Alphidius to the fact that in it there are analogies to all kinds of animals and stones, to all colours and odours, and all the works of men, either manual or mental. Melvescindus adds, that if we call it spiritual we are right; if we describe it as corporal, we are not mistaken; if we style it heavenly, we do not lie; if we call it earthly we say the truth. Lilium avers that our Stone has as many names as there are things, or names of things.

Alphidius says: In our Magistery there is a great abundance of parables, names, and similitudes for the purpose of hiding the truth from the ignorant and revealing it to the wise. Morienus delivers himself to the same effect.

The consequence of this great multiplicity of names is that our Stone has really no proper name of its own, by which it is generally known, except this one sufficiently vague and indefinite name of Philosopher's Stone. This appellation being hardly sufficiently representative of the qualities of our Stone, each individual Sage has invented one or more names of his own, of which the appropriateness is patent only to those who are acquainted with the facts to which they refer. They are generally derived from some process or change of colour which our substance undergoes in the course of our Magistery. The substance indeed is one, but just as gold being worked up into different shapes is called by different names, such as ring, bracelet, crown, etc., though in substance all these are nothing but gold; so our one substance comes to bear different names derived from the changes to which it is subjected. In the same way as ordinary men in common parlance express their meaning proverbially and metaphorically, clothing a plain thought in figurative language, so our Sages find it necessary to describe this secret of secrets, and mystery of mysteries, in figurative terms, so that it may remain a profound arcanum to the wicked, the arrogant, the profane, and all to whom God Himself will not permit it to be revealed.

REFUTATIONS OF THE OBJECTIONS TO ALCHEMY.

THE FOREGOING DISTINCTIONS AND DECLARATIONS HAVING BEEN SET FORTH, TO THE GREAT ELUCIDATION OF THE WHOLE SUBJECT, WE WILL NOW PROCEED TO REFUTE THE ARGUMENTS ALLEGED AGAINST THE TRUTH OF OUR ART, AT THE SAME TIME GIVING SUCH ILLUSTRATIONS AND EXPLANATIONS AS MAY SUGGEST THEMSELVES.

IT is hoped that what has been said has supplied the reader with all desirable information with regard to the scope and bearing of our Art. We now propose to say something in refutation of the arguments intended to discredit Alchemy in the eyes of those who suppose themselves to be learned.

Refutation of the First Five Objections.

The fact is that, in producing gold, the Art of Alchemy does not pretend to imitate the whole work of Nature. It does not create metals, or even develop them out of the metallic first-substance; it only takes up the unfinished handiwork of Nature (*i.e.*, the imperfect metals), and completes it (transmutes metals into gold). It is not then necessary that Nature's mode of operation, or the proportion of elements, or their mixture, or the proper time and place, should be so very accurately known to the Artist. For Nature has only left a comparatively small thing for him to do—the completion of that which she has already begun. Moreover, our Artists do not, as a matter of fact, set to work without having first investigated Nature's method of procedure. Nature herself is set upon changing these metals into gold; the Artist has only to remove the cause which hinders this change (*i.e.*, the corrupting sulphur), and then he can depend upon Nature for the rest. This matter will, however, be more clearly explained below in our chapters on the generation of metals. As to the brief space of time required for the conversion in our Art, it must not be thought that we bring this about by exposing metals in the furnace to the sudden operation of fierce heat. If we did so, their metallic moisture would, of course, be destroyed and dried up. But we only just melt the imperfect metals over the fire, and then add to them the Philosopher's Stone, which, in a moment of time, imparts to them the form of gold, thus changing and ennobling their nature, and conserving their own proper metallic humour. It would not be possible for us to evolve gold and silver out of the metallic first-substance; but with the help of our Stone, in a fire sufficient for liquefaction, preserving the moisture and removing the superfluity, do we generate that volatile Stone which we seek, to which we unite our fixed Red Stone, and then we can very easily hasten and facilitate an inward action which Nature has already set going, which alone has been brought to a standstill by the presence of impure sulphur.

It is a frequent cause of error to

reason about some particular fact or facts in vague and general terms. Where particulars are concerned, you ought to confine your syllogism to the same category, or we may be logically compelled to admit what we know to be nonsense. Now, if you look at the five first arguments directed against our Art, you will find that they are all couched in the most indefinite language; and, therefore, until our opponents descend to matter-of-fact particulars, we cannot consent to regard their arguments as deserving of a refutation.

Refutation of the Sixth Objection.

In our Magistery there are two things to be taken into account—the action of Nature, and the ministration of our Art. In respect of the first consideration—the indwelling natural agent—the whole work from beginning to end is, of course, brought about by it, and by it alone: the digestion, conjunction, generation, and formation of our Blessed Stone are due to it. Nevertheless, there is another point of view, in which our Magistery may be termed an artificial process; without its aid the action of Nature could either not go on at all, or would not be accomplished with so great rapidity. But the moving principle in our Art is undoubtedly natural, and the same must be true of its products. In a word, generation and combination are natural, but the ministration is the work of art, being in Alchemy even as in the cooking of food.

Refutation of the Seventh Objection.

In this argument of our opponents the conclusion is invalid because the form, which is the perfection of a thing, is twofold, one in so far as it is mixed, and one in so far as it has the principle of life and development, or has such a principle introduced from without by means of the quintessence, or in some other way. In the case of animate objects, the nobler part of the composition is often this vital principle; with inanimate objects, indeed, the reverse is naturally the case. For this reason we cannot form a lion, a goat, or a man;

for though we might know the exact composition of their bodies, yet it is impossible for us ever to understand the evolution of the soul. In like manner, though we are familiar with the generation of some minerals, vegetables, and animals, yet we are ignorant of their specific forms. But in the generation of gold, we know the specific form or composition, separated from the perfectible matter, and the methods of perfection and conjunction, according to Nature. The specific form of the common metals is, as a matter of fact, the same as that of gold and silver. There is no need for us to create metals; we only remove certain impurities which stand in the way of their development, and they then become commuted into gold and silver of their own accord.

Refutation of the Eighth Objection.

This objection is not conclusive because the metals, as has been said, differ not specifically, but only accidentally. But this objection will be more irrefragably refuted below, when we deal at some length with the argument advanced by Aristotle.

Refutation of the Ninth Objection.

It is true that the generation of some earthly things is dependent on the influences and movements of heavenly bodies, for the introduction of their form, but it is not needful for us to know of them, nor indeed is it possible, except in a confused way, as, for example, in the seasons of the year which are caused by the movements of the sun, and determine the sowing and the growth of plants, with the sexual commerce of horses, asses, hawks, falcons, etc., which are capable of producing offspring only at certain periods of the solar year. But the rule does not apply to men, pigeons, and fowls. If we wish to generate worms in a putrefying body, we need not attend to the season of the year, but only to certain conditions of warmth, etc., which it is easy for us to bring about by artificial means. In the same way, a certain degree of equable warmth will always hatch the eggs of the domestic hen. The same principle may be observed in the generation of lime, vitriol, salt, and so on. To operations of this kind the heavenly influences appear to be always favourable; and all Sages are unanimous in saying that our Magistery belongs to this class, because it may be performed at any time or period of the year. It is only indispensable, says Rhasis, that all other necessary conditions should be properly fulfilled, and then the stellar influences will not be wanting. And this dictum is substantially confirmed by Lilium and others. So also Plato states that the celestial influences are poured down according to the value of the matter. Wherever, indeed, it is necessary to infuse a new accidental form, the sites, aspects, and conjunctions of the heavenly bodies must be carefully observed. But as the Art of Alchemy makes no demand of this kind, the knowledge required for such an operation is not needed.

Refutation of the Tenth Objection.

Forms are either natural or artificial; and natural forms are either substantial or accidental. The substantial form is that which makes a thing what it is, and differentiates it from all other objects of the same genus. It is also called the specific form. The accidental form embraces all the proper manifestations of the substantial or specific form, such as the active and passive qualities of any given object, and its colour, smell, taste, and shape. Artificial forms are entirely accidental, and are nothing but the shapes and qualities imparted to anything by art through the will of the artist, such as the shape of a house, or ship, or coin. Some of these artificial accidents are permanent, as, for instance, a house or a ship; some pass away with the act in which they consist, as, for instance, dancing and singing, and all successive actions. The generation of the Philosopher's Stone is brought about through the mediation or agency of Nature, using the natural instrument of fire, with the natural colour, smell, and shape thereof, which are its accidental forms, following its determined substantial form, but at the same time by means of the artist's aiding hand. Its form is necessarily natural and substantial, and is known by its natural accidental qualities, like everything else in the world. Some assistance is indeed given to the development of the inherent principle; but the inward agent is natural, and the form which is brought into existence by it is also natural, and not artificial, as is falsely asserted by our opponents. Hence the gold which is obtained by means of our Stone, differs in no respect from natural gold, because its form is natural and not artificial.

In order fully to understand the refutation of this tenth objection, we should further consider that natural forms are evolved in two ways. Either Nature supplies the substance and works it up into a given specific form in the absence of any aid from without, or natural substances are combined and prepared in a certain way by art, and then attain to perfection by means of a natural operation. To this latter class belong most chemical compounds. Though here Nature cannot herself prepare and combine the requisite ingredients, yet the result could never be brought about by a merely artificial operation, and is due to Nature alone. Health is restored to the body by Art, but the real agent is Nature, Art only supplying the necessary conditions under which Nature is to work. There is all the difference in the world between an artificial product of this kind and a real artificial product, such as a house, a ship, and the like. Natural products admit of but little variety, and the gold which is produced by Nature, either in the one or the other of the ways indicated above, will always be the same gold. Hence the gold of Alchemy, which is due to a natural process, rendered possible and assisted by Art, is evidently not wanting either in the specific form or the accidental properties of gold found in mines. The principle of Art is Nature, and, after all, the works of

Nature are the operations of Supreme Intelligence, and natural conditions may be established by the intelligent mind of the Artist.

Refutation of the Eleventh Objection.

Our assailants say that it is easier to destroy than to construct. But Geber tells us that what is difficult to construct is also difficult to disintegrate; the stronger the composition of anything, the more difficult is also its decomposition. The making or construction of a thing may be considered in a twofold aspect. There is the initial development of a thing out of its first principles, as, for instance, the blood in the uterine veins of the hen, out of which the egg is formed; then the development of the chicken out of the egg by subjecting it to the warmth of the hen for a certain period, when all necessary conditions of this development already pre-exist in the egg. We may also distinguish a third operation, viz., the laying of the egg by the hen. The change brought about by Alchemy is of the second description. For in the common metals all the necessary conditions of gold are already found, just as the chicken is already contained in the egg. It is not the business of the Alchemist either to know or to put together the component elements of gold. Rather, we may say that he has them in an unfinished state, and commutes them into gold by a process similar to that which changes an egg into a chicken. The twelfth and thirteenth objections are already met by what has been advanced in our previous arguments.

Refutation of the Fourteenth Objection.

To the fourteenth objection, which asserts that it is impossible that the same thing should operate in two contrary ways, we answer that this is true of the same thing, but not true of different things; and this diversity depends on the thing receiving rather than on the thing received. In the human body, for instance, the same agent changes very different foods into the chyme and blood of exactly the same composition, hard food being softened and soft food hardened. Galen tells us that both cold and warm foods ultimately produce animal heat in the body. Considered as foods, all these substances are different, yet they are all turned to the same use by the one agent which we call the vital power. In the same way, the common metals, which are dug out of mines, differ from each other as to the hardness or softness of their composition, and the degree of their purity, etc.; yet they are all subject to the same natural digestion and the inherent action of the same specific form is developing them all in the same direction. In this case, too, through the operation of one and the same force, the hard substances are softened and the soft substances rendered hard, so that both are reduced to one intermediate degree of consistency. Would it not be absurd to say, as is nevertheless asserted by some who are wise in their own conceits, that it is impossible for our Stone to change both copper or lead and iron into gold, because the one is hard and the other soft. It is the digestive power of metals, and it deals with them as the digestive power of the human stomach is able to deal with food. There is, then, as Geber says, in our Magistery only one thing which changes all metals into the same precious substance, viz., the Red Tincture, and this assertion involves no contradiction in terms, as has been supposed on account of the diversity of the common metals. This one medicine hardens that which is soft, and softens that which is hard, fixes that which is fugitive (or volatile), and glorifies them all with its own magnificent brilliancy and splendour. The true artist knows the causes of the hardness of metals, as well as of their softness, the causes of their fusibility, whether that process be quickly or slowly accomplished, and the causes of their fixation and volatility; he is acquainted also with the causes of the perfection of metals, and of their corruption, of all their defects and superfluities; and, therefore, has all the knowledge which our Magistery requires and presupposes.

Refutation of the Fifteenth Objection.

The refutation of this argument is sufficiently patent from what has already been said.

Refutation of the Sixteenth Objection.

It is advanced that common metals are perfect in their own species, and that it is, therefore, impossible to bring them to any higher degree of perfection, just as a horse can never be perfected into a man. But there is such a thing as specific completeness which, nevertheless, admits of a higher development. An egg, for instance, as far as it goes, is specifically complete in itself; and yet it is not perfect as regards the intention of Nature, until it has been digested by means of natural heat into a bird. It would be absurd to say that an egg must always remain an egg, because as such it has certain well-defined properties and a substantial form of its own. The same holds good with regard to the seeds of plants, which are specifically complete as seeds, yet Nature nevertheless designs them to be perfected into living plants. In the same way, tin, lead, and iron, are perfect in their own species, yet in another sense are not perfect, are at once noble and ignoble, and still have not yet achieved the highest possibilities of their nature. The delay in their development is caused by Nature for the sake of man, because the common metals can be turned into uses for which gold and silver could not be employed.

Refutation of the Seventeenth Objection.

The solution of this difficulty is patent from that which has already been said.

Refutation of the Eighteenth and Nineteenth Objections.

Here, too, we may partly refer the reader back to what has already been proved, and partly we must ask him to wait until we deal with the five arguments of Aristotle.

Refutation of the Twentieth Objection.

We are told that the subject matter

of this Art must be contingent, and dependent upon chance rather than upon the strict sequence of natural causes and effects, because the Sages themselves admit that it has never become known to any very considerable number even of its most diligent students. Hence it is asserted that our Art cannot aspire to be a science, and can never, at the very best, be more than a system of haphazard guess work. But it is a mistake to suppose that that which happens only seldom, must therefore necessarily be subject to chance. If our objectors only knew our Art, they would readily admit that it is governed by as rigid a system of unchangeable laws as the most exact science in the world.

We will now proceed to answer the Five Arguments of Aristotle.

As to the first, it has already been met by our proof that the transmutation of metals in Alchemy is brought about by a natural process.

The same remark holds good of the second objection. A solution of his third difficulty has also been given when we proved that it is not necessary for the artist to be acquainted with the exact composition, or substantial and pre-existent form, either of the common metals or of gold and silver, since the necessary process of change is brought about, not by the artist but by the inward natural principle, which strives to fulfil the intention of Nature with regard to it. It is enough to be acquainted with their accidents, properties, and passions, which are the consequence of their form. When any transmuted metal is found to have the properties and passions of mineral gold, without superabundance and without deficiency, we conclude of necessity that it has also the form of gold. It is, of course, impossible, and always will be impossible, for any one to know things by means of their forms, because they do not fall within the cognisance of our senses. That which does the work, and performs the functions, of an eye is an eye, but nothing else really deserves this name; hence a stone or a wax eye is not an eye, but only the similitude of an eye, because it does not perform the functions of an eye. I affirm, notwithstanding, that, among composite things, the form of gold and the Stone of the Philosophers alone can be properly known through the perfect knowledge or cognition of the immediate matter which underlies the visible accidents, which, if the same do not subtend, then is the form unknown and inoperable, as in other composites. There is, however, no need for us to know the forms of common metals; for us it is sufficient to be aware that all metals are in course of development into gold, through the properties and accidents in the immediate first matter, and are capable of being endowed with the form of gold. Whosoever is ignorant of the form in a given matter is ignorant of the possibility of its transmutation, and must judge by his knowledge of accidents and qualities; and, seeing that the gold of the mine and the gold produced by alchemy have precisely the same properties in appearance, and endure the same tests, we conclude that they are both real gold, and are impressed with the same form. The fourth objection of the philosopher has already been met by what has been said above concerning the proportion in which the elements are mixed in any given thing.

We will now attempt to answer the Fifth Objection of Aristotle.

Aristotle obliges us to confess that metals differ not only in their accidents, but specifically, and therefore his argument requires to be answered at some length. Now, there is this difference between potentiality and actuality, that the one is related to the other as non-existence to existence. The potential becomes the actual, the imperfect the perfect, and substance becomes form; but the process is never reversed. Seed is never potentially blood, nor blood potentially food, nor food potentially the four elements. Not everything that is changed into something else is called the substance of that other thing; a living body is not the substance of a corpse, nor wine of vinegar. In the generation of metals all common metals are potentially what gold is actually, they are imperfectly what gold is perfectly; they are substantially what gold is formally. This is evident from the fact—which shall be proved later on—that Nature changes all metals into gold, while gold is never changed into any of the other metals. Hence, if our Art is to succeed it must follow the course of Nature, and do as it is taught by Nature.

It must be further distinguished that in this connection potentiality is of two kinds disposition towards the form and the faculty of receiving form. The first may be divided into approximate, remote, and remotest. The second is also duplex. Now, complete goodness or perfection is one, and amongst the metals there is only one which is good and perfect, namely gold, and gold does not need to go through any change to make it good and perfect. To be perfect is for anything to have realised the ultimate intention of Nature concerning it; the common metals have not yet realised this ideal; hence it still remains for them to be changed into gold. And, as that which is nearest to perfection is the best among imperfect things, silver comes next after gold, then bronze, then tin, then copper, then lead, then iron—as appears from what has been said above.

Gold alone among metals has, therefore, reached the highest stage of actual perfection. All other metals are only potentially perfect. Some of them, however, have left behind the more remote grades of potentiality, and the change they require to undergo is inconsiderable, because their distance from the highest stage of metallic actuality is not very great. We do not affirm, with other writers, that the intention of Nature has been frustrated or arrested in the imperfect metals. We affirm that they are produced in accordance with her intention, and that they are in course of development into gold. This operation is performed either by Nature in the bowels of the earth, or, in an infinitely shorter space of time, by our most glorious Magistery.

There are also three kinds of perfection and imperfection :—(1) Among things which have the same substantial form; (2) among things which have different substantial forms; (3) among things which are in course of development into the same form. The first kind of perfection belongs to a man who has the complete use of all his organs, senses, and faculties; a man who suffers from any defect in these particulars is not so perfect a specimen of humanity. The second kind of perfection is comparative, when we place two things, which are complete in their own species, side by side. So, for instance, a man is a more perfect creature than a horse, and a horse is more perfect (or noble) than an ass. The third kind of perfection we find only amongst those things of the same kind which are in different stages of development towards a certain highest point. This is the species of perfection we refer to when we speak of metals. Each metal differs from all the rest, and has a certain perfection and completeness of its own; but none, except gold, has reached that highest degree of perfection of which it is capable. For all common metals there is a transient and a perfect state of inward completeness, and this perfect state they attain either through the slow operation of Nature, or through the sudden transformatory power of our Stone. We must, however, add that the imperfect metals form part of the great plan and design of Nature, though they are in course of transformation into gold. For a large number of very useful and indispensable tools and utensils could not be provided at all if there were no copper, iron, tin, or lead, and if all metals were either silver or gold. For this beneficent reason Nature has furnished us with the metallic substance in all its different stages of development, from iron, or the lowest, to gold, or the highest state of metallic perfection. Nature is ever studying variety, and, for that reason, instead of covering the whole face of the earth with water, has evolved out of that elementary substance a great diversity of forms, embracing the whole animal, vegetable, and mineral world. It is, in like manner, for the use of men that Nature has differentiated the metallic substance into a great variety of species and forms.

Nevertheless, the great process of development into silver and gold is constantly going on. This appears from the fact that miners often find solid pieces of pure silver in tin and lead mines, and also from the experience of others who have met with pure gold in metallic veins of iron—though this latter occurrence is more rarely observed, on account of the great impurity of iron. In some silver mines, again, quantities of solid gold have been discovered, as, for instance, in Servia; at first, the whole appears to be silver, but in the refiner's crucible the gold is subsequently separated from the less precious metal. Thus it is the teaching of experience that Nature is continually at work changing other metals into gold, because, though, in a certain sense, they are complete in themselves, they have not yet reached the highest perfection of which they are capable, and to which Nature has destined them—just as the human embryo and the little children are complete and perfect as far as they go, but have not yet attained to their ultimate goal of manhood. Gold is found in different forms, either mixed with a coarse rocky substance, or in a solid condition, or amongst the sand in the beds of rivers, being washed out of the mines by water. Golden sand is also found in the deserts of India, where there are no rivers. Silver is never found mixed with the sand of rivers, but mostly in the shape of ore in mines, or like a vein running through a rock. Lead and tin occur mostly in the shape of ore, and sometimes they are mingled with earth. The same facts have been commonly observed with regard to iron and the other metals. When different metals are discovered in the same mine, the less pure of the two will generally be found uppermost, because in the digestion of the metallic substance the impure elements have a tendency to ascend and leave what remains more force to develop in the right direction. The difference between metals, then, may be called specific; but it is not the same difference as that which exists between a horse and a man; it is rather a difference of development, or of the degree of digestion. The common metals have the same metallic form as gold; but the digestion of gold is complete, while that of the others is still more or less imperfect. Thus, there is nothing left for us to do except to continue the digestive process until gold is reached, and so finish it: there is no need for us to reduce the common metals to their first substance, to revert them to the principle of digestion, or to accomplish any other difficult feat of the kind. If, indeed, a horse were to be changed into a man, it would be necessary, by corruption and disintegration, to convert the lower animal form into the first substance, and from this first substance to evolve human seed. Such an operation is, of course, impossible, and to attempt it would be to court failure. Art, therefore, follows Nature in that which it would accomplish after the manner of Nature, and it extols Nature wonderfully, not by violating Nature, but by governing her. But far different is the case of metals, which are all naturally in a state of transition and development into gold. In our Art the metals are not, indeed, changed back into their first substance; but by the juxtaposition and influence of the Blessed Stone, and its subtle mingling with all, even the smallest, parts of the base metal, the Stone, which is the substantial form of gold, impresses this form on every atom of the lead or copper, and thereby transmutes it into gold. This mingling cannot take place, however, without a preliminary melting or liquefaction, which renders the base metal accessible in all its parts to the subtle influence of the Stone, and to the transmuting power of the transmuting medicine. The form which is thus introduced is not accidental, but substantial; and, therefore, the gold which results is not artificial, but natural and real.

Even if it be true, as is generally assumed, that all things are evolved out of the four elements, this theory in no way conflicts with the claims of our Art. For this first substance is not available for any special purpose, unless it has first been changed into a suitable and specifically differentiated form. Thus it is impossible for us to generate a man out of the four elements: for this purpose we must have them in the more specific form of human seed. But where there is human seed, a man may be generated from it without first changing it back into the four elements; rather, the digestion of those four elements, which has already begun, must be continued until the substance assumes the human form. So we cannot produce metals out of the four elements; we must have a viscous, heavy, intermediate water mingled with subtle sulphureous earth, which is the special metallic first substance—that is, quicksilver. This substance, then, through the agency of the sulphur, is developed into gold, or into some common metal, and then into gold. In order to effect this ultimate change, there is no need to reduce the common metals to their first matter, for they already contain that proximate first matter, which may, by comparison, be called the seed of gold, which also has in itself the principle of ultimate development into gold. In the working of Nature there is no regression; we cannot change the embryo back into the seed, nor the seed into the four elements. The common metals are a substance intermediate between gold and silver, on the one hand, and quicksilver and sulphur on the other. Seeing, then, that the middle must always be nearer to the end than is the beginning, therefore the imperfect metals are nearer to gold than is the first matter; and, consequently, it must be easier to obtain gold from the common metals than from a more remote, or less developed substance, like quicksilver and sulphur.

If we say that the common metals are an intermediate substance, and represent the different stages of transition from quicksilver to gold, this remark must be understood to apply to the natural aspect of the process. As far as our Art is concerned, there is a difference both in the arrangement and in the time. Our Stone perfects the quicksilver of the common metals by purifying and partly eliminating their sulphur; and this process of digestion, which may occupy ages in the bowels of the earth, is accomplished by our Stone in a moment of time, on account of the high degree of digestion possessed by our Stone. This elaborate discussion of the arguments for and against our Art was composed by Master Peter Bonus, of Ferrara, in the year of our Lord 1338. The Master was at that time residing in Pola, a township of Istria.

Philosophy of Alchemy.

Now we have established the truth of this Art, we must see to which part of Philosophy it belongs, and how Art and Nature differ and agree.

THERE are three parts of Philosophy: that which deals with matter in motion, or physics; that which is concerned with matter at rest, or mathematics; and that which abstracts from both matter and motion, or metaphysics. Alchemy belongs neither to the second nor to the third of these departments of science; consequently, it takes its place in the first department, or that of physical science, for it deals with real being joined to motion and matter, and not with metaphysics, which are divine, and have regard to real being separated from motion and matter. Each physical science deals with a certain division of matter, and so does our Magistery.

Science is possible by means of the fact that the universe is the work of an Intelligence to which our reason corresponds. The Divine Intelligence has subjected all natural and supernatural phenomena to the rule of certain laws, which laws our reason was created capable of apprehending, and this state of things is the preliminary condition of all science whatsoever. Our reason is either practical or speculative, according to the class of mundane relations with which it deals; and thus we have speculative philosophy, or science, and practical philosophy, or art. Our Magistery is speculative in so far as it teaches us the nature and relations of metals; it is practical in so far as it teaches us how to utilise this knowledge for the production of the Philosopher's Stone, and the transmutation of common metals into gold and silver.

As a department of physical science,

our Art must deal with a certain determinate division of matter; and if our gold is to be identical with that of Nature, it is clear that our Art must follow Nature in this respect, and that it must be concerned with the same matter which Nature employs in the production of gold and silver; otherwise our gold would be specifically, or even generically, different from that of Nature. Now, according to all natural philosophers and all alchemists, this matter is quicksilver; consequently, Alchemy must be concerned in the elaboration of the same material; and, as no matter forms or perfects itself, but is developed and moulded by its own proper agent, so this quicksilver is digested, developed, and moulded, in Nature as in Art, by an inherent agent of its own which we call sulphur, and by which the generation of metals and of gold is accomplished. This sulphur coagulates the said quicksilver and digests it, by its inherent virtue, and by means of its own natural mineral heat. This process of digestion produces a given metal as an intermediate result, but the ultimate aim of the digestive process is gold. In our Art we must have the same quicksilver and the same digestive sulphur as that which brings about the perfection of metals in Nature. But the mode of action, and digestion, and information is different in our Art from that employed by Nature; while, similarly, there is a difference in the local and temporal conditions, but the end is identical. Those, then, who are at work on minerals which are not metals, or on vegetable or animal substances, are spending their labour in vain; for none of these things possess that aptitude and predisposition to become gold which is inherent in all metallic substances.

From all these considerations we see that our Art is in perfect accordance with Nature, and that in most of its conditions it imitates Nature. Hence our gold is fully identical in every essential respect with the gold of Nature, and abides all the tests to which it can possibly be subjected. It contains no impurity of any kind, but its perfect quality is made evident by the examination of fire, whence it follows that it is gold true and natural, form for form and quality for quality. As a fact, it is purer and more precious even than natural gold.

We must now proceed to discuss the first principles of metals, both generally and with particular reference to our Art, and to the procreation and transmutation of metals. The student should remember that, while poring over the pages of Alchemistic books, he should not neglect the practical side of our Art, because it is practice which both explains the difficulties of speculative truth and corrects any speculative error that may happen to arise.

The Prime Principles of Metals.

Namely, of the first substances of metals in general, and of their generation and mutual transmutation according to Nature; and how and by what methods Art can follow Nature.

ALL metals are proved to belong to the same species by their coagulation, by their one mode of commixtion, and by their capacity of retaining their specific properties both when they are melted and when they are coagulated. Hence their matter is one, viz., a humid and watery matter, and it is natural for such a substance to go on in its development till it is completely fixed. As water quickly evaporates over the fire, while the humidity of metals is capable of enduring great heat without evaporation, this humidity cannot be water only, but is water mixed with, and modified by, other elements. Moreover, there must be something else which gives to this viscous and unctuous water that humidity and consistency which we observe in metals, viz., the modification introduced by their earthy ingredients.

Thus, in the generation of metals, we distinguish two kinds of moisture, one of which is viscous and external, and not totally joined to the earthy parts of the substance; and the same is inflammable and sulphureous; while the other is a viscous internal humidity, and is identical in its composition with the earthy portions; it is neither combustible nor inflammable, because all its smallest parts are so intimately joined together as to make up one inseparable quicksilver: the dry and the moist particles are too closely united to be severed by the heat of fire, and there is a perfect balance between them.

The first matter of all metals, then, is humid, viscous, incombustible, subtle, incorporated, in the mineral caverns, with subtle earth, with which it is equally and indissolubly mixed in its smallest particles. The proximate matter of metals is quicksilver, generated out of their indissoluble commixtion. To this Nature, in her wisdom, has joined a proper agent, viz., sulphur, which digests and moulds it into the metallic form. Sulphur is a certain earthy fatness, thickened and hardened by well-tempered decoction, and it is related to quicksilver as the male to the female, and as the proper agent to the proper matter. Some sulphur is fusible, and some is not, according as the metals to which it belongs are also fusible or not. Quicksilver is coagulated in the bowels of the earth by its own proper sulphur. Hence we ought to say that these two, quicksilver and sulphur, in their joint mutual operation, are the first principle of metals. The possibility of changing common metals into gold lies in the fact that in ordinary metals the sulphur has not yet fully done its work; for if they were perfect as they are, it would be necessary to change them back into the first metallic substance before transmuting them into gold; and this has been admitted to be impossible.

Nature, then, has two ways of producing gold; either it changes the quicksilver at once into the precious metal, or it develops it first into iron, lead, copper, etc., and then into gold. Art follows Nature in adopting her second method; but as regards the first, it is impossible for our Art to imitate Nature. These two methods are the mediate and the immediate; but the mediate must become the immediate before it is available for the purposes of our Art. Our Art thoroughly purges the common metals of all the impure and corrupt sulphur which they contain, so that the development of the quicksilver can go on unhindered. If any Artist had such cunning as to change back animal and vegetable substances into their first elements, it might be possible for him to evolve gold in this way: but this feat necessarily lies beyond the reach of human ingenuity, and, therefore, the Artist who is busied with animal and vegetable matter, is wasting both time, money, and trouble. Geber, towards the end of his chapter on medicines of the first order, tells us that all alterant medicines are derived either from quicksilver, sulphur, a mixture of the two, or of some things possessing their nature, and no change can be encompassed without their agency. For this reason we must depend on them, and on them alone, for bringing about the conversion which we contemplate as desirable. The perfection of philosophical quicksilver is the purification of its agent (or sulphur) from all corrupting influences by means of our Art; and so the two together perform what each by itself was unable to accomplish—because each was separated from the other, and hindered from doing its work by certain deadly impurities. Art imitates the method of Nature in bringing about this purification, both in the generation of the Philosophical Stone and in the perfecting of metals. The exact way in which the purification is accomplished is different, especially because it is much shorter; but the principle is the same. If Nature did not change common metals into gold, all the efforts of the alchemist's Art would be vain.

Now we can give a solution of the difficulties suggested in Objections Nos. 18 and 19.

Nature cannot accomplish the work of our Art, *i.e.*, the production of the Philosopher's Stone. Art, on the other hand, cannot follow as closely as many have thought in the footsteps of Nature, though it accomplishes the same work of perfecting metals. But both Art and Nature are governed by an equally prevailing principle, and the results are the same in both cases, though there may be a difference in the intermediate stages of the two processes. This is our answer to the eighteenth objection. The answer to the nineteenth objection is equally obvious, because the generation of gold according to Nature and of this gold according to our Art is, in substance, one and the same process, consisting in the purification of the active sulphur. Though the processes preceding the ultimate change are different in our Art from those employed by Nature, the ultimate result itself is identical in both cases. Thus, even if the same change which is produced by our Stone could be produced by some other medicine, the result would still be pure gold. Only this is impossible, for all Alchemy pleads aloud in favour of our Stone as the only possible Alterative Remedy of the mineral world. For there is no real connection between vegetable and animal sulphur, etc., and metallic or even mineral substances.

It should be noted that the sulphur hidden in the quicksilver is that which imparts the form of the gold, by virtue of the heat of the mineral gold and the external sulphur; hence the gold colour, which we observe in some other metals, does not justify us in calling them gold.

There is, indeed, a kind of gold which has been made of silver, reduced to the density of gold, by some pretending to a knowledge of Alchemy, which also endures all the ordinary tests, except that it is not sufficiently soft to be malleable; that it is devoid of the true fusible quality; that it has not the clear ring of gold; and that it does not absorb quicksilver with sufficient rapidity; moreover it is not possible to aureate metals therewith. But this observation shews that the ordinary tests of the assayer are delusive, and that there is such a thing as a substance which an assayer would pronounce to be gold, which yet is not real gold. This remark, however, does not apply to the gold of the alchemists, for it not only endures all the ordinary tests, but is like other gold in all respects whatsoever. The matter would wear a very different aspect if we attempted to prepare our Stone from some vegetable substance, because no vegetable substance could possibly be the means of producing real gold.

The Generation of Metals.

Of the First Principles of Metals in particular, and of their Generation according to the intention of Nature; of the signs of this Generation, shewing how Art must follow Nature in having similar outward signs, and the same First Principles, in the generation of the Philosopher's Stone. Herein is contained the whole Secret of Nature.

IF two things generally belong together, and if one of them is sometimes found apart, the other will also be sometimes found apart. For instance, that which is moved and that which moves form a pair; if that which is moved occurs by itself, that which moves must also be found by itself. We have seen that quicksilver and sulphur are the first principles of metals, and that the former is developed by the latter. When the sulphur has done its work for the quicksilver, it is separated from it, so that the quicksilver remains by itself. It follows that the sulphur must also be by itself. If, at the end of the digestive process, the sulphur remains mixed with the quicksilver, the result will be one of the base metals. Art, following in the footsteps of Nature, takes the same substance, and as Nature, at the end of her work, separates off the sulphur, and imparts to the quicksilver in an instant the form of gold, leaving the sulphur on one side, so Art must, in all essential points, follow the guidance of Nature. When the artist sees the quicksilver in a separate condition, he knows that the sulphur is also by itself. This separation must take place if the Philosopher's Stone is to be evolved, and then the substance will receive its form at its own proper time, as assigned to it by Nature. *Note that we have here the whole Secret of Nature and the Art.*

Every solid substance, like wood, stone, etc., is bounded by its proper limits, because its solidity gives it power to retain its own shape. But water, oil, and all liquids are bounded by something else. So our metallic humour is at first bounded by something else; but when it becomes perfectly solid and fixed, it also is bounded by its own limits.

Note with regard to the Quicksilver, etc., etc.

When quicksilver is first used in our Magistery, it is bounded by something else; but if we would retain it, we should take care to enclose it within its own limits, *i.e.*, to coagulate it with its earthy parts, and not with foreign substances.

Note in regard to the Conversion of the Elements.

Then the elements are changed one into another, water into earth, and air into fire. For its earthy parts are nothing but the hidden gold of the Sages, also called the "Body," or "Ferment," or "Poison." Moreover, when digestion is complete, it is made evident by the separation of all superfluous and corrupting sulphur, at which point the operation should finish.

Note with regard to the superfluous Sulphur, etc.

At the beginning of the process of digestion there were two kinds of superfluous sulphur, of which the first was subtle and combustible. By means of the evaporation in the sublimation this sulphur is separated from the quicksilver. But there is another gross, earthy, and feculent sulphur, which sinks to the bottom of the vessel, over which is the pure, volatile substance. For as in the digestion of must and blood there is separated therefrom a subtle and a gross superfluous substance, and the pure liquid is between the two, so, in our work, there is a fiery and subtle, and a gross and earthy, sulphureous superfluity. This separation is brought about by digestion or coction, supervised by Art, which prevents the volatile elements from escaping. So long as the sulphur remains joined to the quicksilver the work is imperfect, just as metals are imperfect under the same conditions, that is, in comparison with gold. This substance is the quicksilver of the Sages, and it permits of being united with glass; in other words, with its body, ferment, poison, or salt. This is that which imbibes glass as a thirsty man drinks cold water; this is the medium of union between Sun and Moon; the same is the electrum of Nature. It is also the fugitive slave, and blessed is he who can overtake him, for his nature adapts itself to all things. This also is called Virgin's milk. The same substance is meant by all these expressions. The colour which appears when the first coction is complete is whiteness; then we know that the quicksilver is fully separated from the sulphur; hence we observe at this stage the brilliant splendour of the quicksilver.

It should, however, be noted that the white colour is easily affected by all other colours in turn, seeing that it readily receives their nature and composition. This susceptibility of the white colour to even a small portion of some other colour may be observed in the dyeing of wool and silk. For whiteness is the element and foundation of all other colours. White substances are equally open to modifications of taste and scent, as, for example, the facility with which the insipid flavour of water may be itself changed by the addition of some more savoury substance. The same rule holds good with the simple atmospheric air, which very easily becomes contaminated by odours. In the case of metals this rule does not obtain, for a small quantity of quicksilver whitens a large portion of gold or copper.

Note as regards the Digestion of Quicksilver.

When by means of our alchemical digestion we obtain quicksilver from the principles of the metals, then is manifested a full and homogeneous whiteness, but we must take care to remember that the orange colour of gold, and the final redness, are both hidden beneath this whiteness. The same will persist till the quicksilver has been overcome, after which the orange and red will replace it. The quicksilver assimilates everything else to its own colour, so long as it is in a liquid state; but its colour is changed as soon as it is coagulated. It is coagulated by the perfecting agent within itself, *i.e.*, that divine sulphur, which appears white so long as the quicksilver is liquid, but imparts to the quicksilver its own red colour as soon as it is coagulated. This divine sulphur is of the nature and form of the Sun (gold), while the quicksilver is of the nature of the Moon (silver). When these two waters are combined, coagulation takes place with a colour of the whiteness of snow; and this whiteness signifies the eternal peace and concord of the elements, and the accomplishment of the Great Work of Alchemy.

Two Secrets: How far also Art is more sublime even than Nature.

Hereby two secrets are revealed to us in our Art. The first is the mode of operation; the second is the material, which is so secret, that, though it be very clearly described, men cannot find it. In Nature there is only one coction;

but as it is necessary to elicit from the white matter the red colour which lies hidden beneath, it is necessary also to have two magisteries, coctions, or digestive processes, in our Art. A mistake is often made in attempting to imitate too closely the exact methods of Nature, instead of following the great principles of Nature only. The form of gold must be imparted to common metals from within, by development, and not from without, by infusion. Those metals which have a larger admixture of sulphur, partake more of the nature of sulphur, while those which have a larger admixture of quicksilver, partake more of the nature of quicksilver. But as sulphur does not mingle with gold, the substance of gold must consist entirely of quicksilver; and since the Philosopher's Stone is the form of gold, and is required to inform the other metals, it must be generated from quicksilver alone. The form of a thing is more noble than the thing itself, and our Stone is, for this reason, more precious than gold. For the form is that which makes a thing what it is.

Of the Form and Matter we obtain a Compound; this Matter is Quicksilver and the Common Metals, and the compound is Gold.

The result of our Magistery is the form of gold. This form by itself would be nothing, because it is unable to manifest its virtues and operations, unless it be combined with some matter, and form a compost therewith; but as it is the form of gold which makes gold what it is, so when our Stone impresses itself upon any common metal, it subtly pervades it with the said form of gold in every smallest part, or, in other words, turns it into gold. Here the substance is quicksilver and the common metals, the form is our Stone, and the resultant compound is gold.

Thus there is only one Stone, both white and red, as all Alchemy testifies; for as the form of all individuals of the same species is one and the same, it follows that the form of all gold is the same, and that there can be only one Stone, because Alchemy sets itself to turn all metals into gold. Notice also that in most metals you find neither quicksilver by itself, nor sulphur by itself, but a mixture of the two which has the power of development into gold. This is the metallic First Matter, and only an ignorant person will look for it in the vegetable or animal world.

Epilogue and Conclusion.

Shewing why the Philosopher denied this Art, and how he subsequently admitted the Secret of Gold-making.

In his fourth book of *Meteorology*, Aristotle explains why he apparently denied the truth of Alchemy. It was this form, he says, which induced the ancient Sages to speak of a form apart from its substance.

He alludes to the Platonists and Pythagoreans, who spoke of forms or ideas as if they existed somewhere in the air, apart from their concrete manifestations, and were imparted from without to combinations of matter disposed in a certain suitable way. This view is opposed by Aristotle, though it seems that Plato spoke figuratively, and was thinking of the operation of our Stone. In the passage which we have quoted, Aristotle certainly appears to understand him in that sense. But in his *Metaphysics*, Aristotle was anxious to uphold his own view with regard to forms in general, and therefore he spoke as he did. He opposed Plato according to the literal sense of his words; but he never for a moment intended to assail their occult and mystical meaning. In his old age the secret became known to him, and therefore he recanted in his last work the opinion which he had apparently set forth in his earlier writings. When he wrote against our Art he was a young man, and was reasoning in a general way; but in his old age he gave the deliberate verdict of his experience, and spoke from particular knowledge. No one is really qualified to pass judgment upon any art or science who knows nothing about it, and is only reasoning from general or universal premises: for nothing is more deceptive than such reasoning, and there is no more frequent or fruitful source of error. Moreover, the opinion of an old man is infinitely more valuable than the haphazard talk of youth, since young men — according to Aristotle himself—are not wise, while wisdom is an attribute of old age. As an old man, Aristotle agreed with the ancient Sages, and was heartily willing to admit that this Art is true, and according to Nature, as he has set forth at length in his *Epistle to King Alexander.*

A Demonstration of Alchemy after Another Manner.

Here follow the reasons shewing, by a different method from that employed above, that the Art of Alchemy is true, and that the Gold of the Stone is purer and more perfect even than Natural Gold.

THE gold and silver produced by our Art are better and purer than those developed in the ordinary way, because alchemical gold is perfectly purged of all sulphureous dross, while natural gold is still blackened, corrupted, and rendered more perishable by the presence of a sulphureous remnant, for which reason also it is somewhat diminished in the fire. Natural gold is still capable of a higher degree of perfection, but our gold is the highest perfection of the metallic substance. Art might give to gold a more intense colouring than Nature, but refrains from doing so, in order not to transcend the bounds of Nature. If the artist knows the two first substances employed by Nature, and Nature's mode of operation, it will also be possible for him to elaborate real gold.

Now we will mention the chief reasons which prove that our gold is, to say the least, as good as the gold of Nature; these arguments will also establish the truth of Alchemy, and its claims.

Every undigested thing capable of digestion, and every impure thing capable of purification, can be digested and expurgated. Now this is the case with iron, lead, copper, tin, etc.; consequently, they can be completely digested, and for any metal to be perfectly pure and digested is to be gold or silver; hence all metals can be changed into gold. As in every digestion there is some superfluity, it must be separated from the substance by means of digestion, because heat brings together things homogeneous and separates things heterogeneous. Outward heat aids the inward or natural digestive heat, and in this way the digestion is accelerated and perfected — as food is better digested if the inward animal heat be aided by warm baths. In the case of fruits, we see that when there is a deficiency of outward heat, they are not properly ripened. This want of inward heat we meet with in all metals except gold; and, in comparison with gold, this is true even of silver. Complete digestion is also called optesis or elixir, while its opposite is described by Aristotle as scatesis or assation. In the case of assation the inward heat is not so completely drawn out by means of moisture as in the case of those metals which are subject to optesis. By digestion, or optesis, as the philosopher informs us, a new metal is formed out of common metals, because the digestion of the substance is now complete. That which begins to generate by means of digestion, must also complete what it has undertaken by means of digestion, because it is the same agent which predisposes to a certain form and imparts the form itself. This agent is Nature, either by herself, or with the aid of Art. Do we not see lead, and gold, and all metals, generated by Nature in mines out of their first principles, viz., quicksilver and sulphur? But this generation is not brought about without a transitional substance intermediate between the softness of quicksilver and the malleable hardness of the metals. This intermediate substance is coagulated, but not purified, and according to the different conditions of digestion, time, place, quality, etc., becomes either gold, or a common metal with a predisposition to be developed into gold. This intermediate matter is that on which our Art sets to work; and it strives to purify and digest it into the form of gold, which can change all other metals into that precious substance. Thus the digestion of our Art is different not in kind but in degree, place, and time, from that of Nature, being as much more perfect as the form of gold is more perfect than gold itself. But if our digestion, and our place, or artificial organ, are at least equal in power to those of Nature, it is clear that the Art of Alchemy is possible, as far as the conditions of place and digestion are concerned. Moreover, our Art must attain better results than Nature, because it can bring a well-regulated supply of outward heat to bear on the material, and this outward heat powerfully aids the inward action. But the very question whether our Art is able to change back gold into one of the common metals is absurd : certainly Nature never attempts anything of the kind. Nor does our Art endeavour to change one imperfect metal into another, since for such a course there is no precedent in Nature. We might indeed change each imperfect metal into the next higher, as Nature may be supposed to do, if we only knew the exact mixture of quicksilver and sulphur required for such a purpose; but as we do not, and shall never know, we can only change imperfect metals into gold, in which, as we are aware, there must be a total absence of impure sulphur. It is quite possible, however, as Geber says, that this change of one imperfect metal into the one next above it may sometimes take place accidentally, through the failure of an attempt to commute them into gold. Another difficulty is propounded by those who fully admit the possibility of imitating the digestive process by which Nature effects the transmutation of common into precious metals; but as Nature requires so many years for that purpose, they do not see how our elixir can bring about the change in a moment of time. We answer that the digestion of gold and of our elixir are alone complete; but whereas gold is a compound, and is only sufficiently digested for its own purposes, the elixir is the form of gold, and its digestion suffices not only for itself, but is so exuberant, and capable of such indefinite multiplication, as to make up in a brief space of time for what is wanting in the common metals. The digestion itself does not take place in a few moments, but has been brought about by the preparation of the Elixir in our Magistery, and is now simply transferred to the common metal in a few moments; moreover, we must not forget to reckon the amount of digestion which has already taken place in the common metal.

And if it be further objected that quicksilver is not half digested like the other metals, but quite crude and undigested, we answer that all the perfection of metals consists in their quicksilver, and that when common metals are perfected, they are cleared of all corrupting sulphur, and only their quicksilver is perfected into gold; as soon as the quicksilver is thus purified, it is of the same nature with the elixir, and can receive some of its exuberant digestion. It is thus very well possible for our Art to imitate Nature in the generation of gold and silver. The whole process is admirably illustrated by Aristotle's remarks in regard to *atramenta*, in the fourth chapter of his *Meteorology*, and we cannot do better than refer the learned reader to that passage. We are here at least convinced that there is no natural process which Art cannot imitate by simply following in the footsteps of Nature and availing itself of every short cut which may be suggested by the opportunity of the case. The chief reason why it is not so easy for Art to imitate Nature lies in the fact that it is sometimes difficult to find the first substance employed by Nature, as Aristotle says in his first book on *Heaven and the World*. The want of material is the chief cause in anything why something like it is not generated. Hence, if Art is to generate the same things as Nature, it must succeed in discovering the exact substance with which Nature works, and must then deal with it according to Nature's methods. Since, then, our Art has found the substance of gold and silver, it is proved to be possible, as far as the substance is concerned. And as our Art possesses also the form of gold and silver, and the combination of the substance and form of anything will produce that thing, it is clear that the Art of Alchemy must possess the secret of producing silver and gold. Moreover, the substance of anything is never found by itself, but always in combination with its form. From this very fact it would follow that if alchemists are really in possession of the substance of our Stone, they must also be able to evolve its form. It is, then, the business of the alchemist to consider the form of metals, both perfect and imperfect, and the two are ultimately found to be both the form and the substance of gold. The proper method of procedure in the proper substance causes the generation of the form in that substance. The substance of common metals is the same as that of gold; if, then, the form of gold, or the elixir, be added to them, they must become gold. As the common metals become gold and silver by means of a natural process, it is quite possible that the same result should be brought about by means of the alchemist's art.

Second Argument.

Whatever has the same causes as some other thing, has also the same accidents, or, in our case, the same composition. Now, the causes of all metals are the same, consequently they all have the same composition. For their matter, their form, and their ultimate destination are the same. They are all equally fusible and malleable, which is not the case with any other substances, and shews that they are all destined to the same ultimate form. There are some substances which resemble metals in all other respects, but are wanting in these two qualities.

Third Argument.

Things which agree in matter are easily changed into each other; now metals answer to this condition, consequently they are mutually transmutable. The reason why they are easily changed into each other is that they are all not very remote from their common first matter, which admits of division into the four elements. Moreover, they all consist of the same matter, viz., quicksilver and sulphur, which again facilitates their mutual transmutation. Amongst metals there is only one that is quite perfect, and represents the highest stage of metallic completeness, namely, gold, and all the others have a predisposition to be changed into it. Hermes Trismegistus says that the inter-generation, transmutation, and conversion of the metals is like that of the elements. If, then, elements are changed into each other, though each is perfect in itself, how much more must this be the case with metals which are all, except gold, in a state of transition towards a more perfect state, especially as metals all have the same matter digested in the same way, which is by no means the case with the elements. Again, when two metals are mixed, the compound still retains all the metallic accidents and properties; but this remark does not hold good with regard to the elements; for their compounds differ very considerably from their simple essences; nor do they mix so easily as metals. Thus it is patent to everyone that the metals must all be classified together, for they only represent different stages of the same thing. The reason that Art imitates Nature is that Nature is governed by a Supreme Intelligence, which has its earthly counterpart in the human Reason, the presiding genius of our Art, as of all Arts. Art brings about new natural conditions, which are not found in Nature, and thus achieves wonders which Nature cannot, or, at any rate, does not, accomplish.

Fourth Argument.

Whatever is in an intermediate stage of development towards something may become that something if its development be not hindered, or if the hindrance be removed. But the imperfect metals are in this state, consequently, etc. An intermediate substance may much more easily attain to perfection than a first substance; for it is already nearer to the final stage of perfection. Aristotle says that there are two ways in which one thing may be developed out of something else; either that thing may be in an intermediate stage, and attain to perfection, *e.g.*, a man may be developed out of a boy, or one extreme may pass into another extreme, *e.g.*, water may become air. The former change is more naturally accomplished than the latter.

Fifth Argument.

Fifthly and lastly, whatever is on the way towards a certain goal may naturally be made to attain that goal; this is the case as regards common metals in respect to gold; consequently, they may be developed into gold. This proposition is clearly established by the fact that all metals are potentially gold.

These reasons, which prove the truth of Alchemy, may be deemed sufficient. As to the rest, it is far easier to forge arguments against anything than to prove the falsity of those arguments, especially in dealing with such a mysterious Art as that of Alchemy.

AN EXCELLENT INTRODUCTION TO THE ART OF ALCHEMY.

TABLE OF THE CONTENTS OF THE FOLLOWING CHAPTERS.

Chapter I.—The Matter of the Philosopher's Stone.
Chapter II.—Is Sulphur the Matter of the Stone?
Chapter III.—The Elements of the Stone and their Composition.
Chapter IV.—The Ferment: its conditions, properties, conversion, etc.
Chapter V.—What is theriac, and the poison of the Stone?
Chapter VI.—The coagulum, the milk, the male and the female of the Stone.
Chapter VII.—Analogy between the generation of gold, the generation of man, and the germination of grain.
Chapter VIII.—Solution of a difficulty with respect to gold and silver, which, it is said, cannot be elaborated from iron

and bronze, by means of the Stone. Special attention should be paid to this solution, as it is of great importance.

These chapters, with the arguments previously determined, are faithfully and diligently compiled from the treatise of Master Peter Bonus, of Ferrara, a concordance of all ancient and modern Sages, forming an excellent introduction to the Art of Alchemy. By him it is named the Precious New Pearl.

Bonus tells us that as beginners we are apt to consider this an easy Art; but as we get to know more about it, we find that we were grievously mistaken in our first impression. On every side we are confronted with so many doubts, difficulties, and apparent contradictions, that we are apt to wonder, after a time, at the youthful rashness and foolhardiness with which we began the study. But in the following chapters we hope to set all difficulties at rest.

Chapter I.

The Matter of the Philosopher's Stone. The Matter of the Metals, and its causes, properties, and qualities.

THE great Geber tells us that metals are substantially composed of quicksilver and sulphur; though sulphur is their active principle rather than part of their substance. Their differences are generally traceable to a difference in the sulphur, which is found white, yellowish, red, saffron-coloured, green, and black, while the quicksilver, considered by itself, is always the same. Sometimes, indeed, the quicksilver has an earthy appearance, but this is owing to an admixture of lead, and can be remedied by a process of purification. Now, as sulphur, which is the proper coagulum of quicksilver, varies in its colour, while quicksilver is always white, it follows that the quicksilver receives its colour from the sulphur, and the sulphur causes the peculiar colour of the different metals. Everything else that is found in metals is more or less impure, and does not really belong to them. It should be noticed that, when metals are mixed, the quicksilver readily combines with quicksilver, because it is the same substance in all metals. But this cannot be said of the sulphur, because it is not the same in all metals.

Note.

Hence, fixed sulphur retards fusion and liquefaction in metals, and entirely prevents it where its quantity exceeds that of the quicksilver. The latter is the case in iron, and the said metal is, therefore, not fusible. This fact we are taught by experience, for when we desire to make fixed sulphur, we must calcine it, and that which is calcined is not susceptible of fusion. But sulphur which is not fixed accelerates fusion, as we see in the case of arsenic, which is of the nature of sulphur, and brings about the fusion of red-hot iron. That it is sulphur which prevents fusion, we see from the fact that when miners smelt ore, there ascends a sulphureous vapour before fusion takes place, and if we collect this substance in a vessel, it is found to resemble orpiment. But both its smell and its properties shew that it consists largely of sulphur. In the same way, fixed sulphur is said to be the cause of the hardness of metals, as we see in iron and brass. Therefore, also, sulphur is the cause of fixation in metals, Sulphur, which is not fixed, on the other hand, is the cause of metallic softness, and of volatilization under the test of fire, as we see in lead and tin. But quicksilver, whether fixed or not, is the cause of metallic fusion. Whatever substances are fused with great difficulty are quickly coagulated (on account of the sulphur which they contain) and *vice versa.*

Sulphur easily adheres to iron and brass, and readily mingles with silver, which has a proportion of combustible sulphur, and also with lead, the latter because lead contains many parts of sulphur which is not fixed. It does not mingle well with tin because of the large quantity of quicksilver which the latter contains. With gold it does not mix at all, because gold is purged of all its sulphur. Quicksilver, on the other hand, enters gold very readily, as it also does silver, and—in a less degree—tin and lead, because of the large quantity of undigested quicksilver contained in them. Brass will receive it with difficulty, and iron not at all, except by an artifice. To tin it adheres on account of its undigested state, and on account of its large quantity of quicksilver. To gold it adheres most easily of all, because gold abounds in quicksilver. The fixed fusible quicksilver, then, is the cause of perfection in metals, and the less fixed it is, the further it is from perfection. Sulphur, on the other hand, whether fixed or volatile, is the cause of corruption and imperfection, so long as it remains in metals. Hence, we conclude that our noble Stone consists of quicksilver exclusively without any trace of external sulphur. This we see from the fact that quicksilver takes to nothing in the whole world more kindly than to gold; nothing, on the other hand, is more unlike gold than sulphur. Whoever denies that quicksilver is the true substance of metals, is like one who says that snow is not white. And because the Stone must enter the metals in all their parts, it is clear that it must consist entirely of quicksilver. Our assertion is borne out by the authority of Rhasis, Alphidius, and Geber. Rhasis, in his *Seventy Precepts*, affirms that Mercury is the root of all things, it only should be prepared, and from it is derived a good tincture, and a strong and conquering impression. Alphidius declares, on the evidence of all the sages, that the work of wisdom consists solely in quicksilver. So also Geber says, in his chapter on the procreation of iron: Let us praise the Blessed, Glorious, and most High God, Who created quicksilver, and gave it a substance, and imparted to its substance properties which no other substance on earth can possess. It is the perfection of our Art, it is our victory which overcomes fire, and is not overcome by it, but delights in its heat, and gently and amicably reposes in it, etc. Though in his book on *The Coagulation of Mercury by Precipitation* he says that this medicine is elicited from metallic bodies with their sulphur and arsenic, he really means the same thing, but he expresses himself somewhat obscurely. We do not, however, need the testimony of the ancients to convince us that quicksilver without external sulphur must be the substance of the Stone, which, as has been said, is the form of gold. The fact is brought home to us with sufficient force by the evidence of our eyes, if, indeed, we have ever observed the facility and amicable readiness with which quicksilver joins itself to gold.

Query: Is sulphur a material part of gold and of our Stone?

But it may be objected that our argument proves too much, and that sulphur must actually form a material part of gold and of the Stone of the Philosophers. If quicksilver must be the matter of the Stone, because it readily unites with gold, we may say with quite as much justice that sulphur must form part of this matter, because it very easily mingles with quicksilver, and especially because sulphur is the proper coagulum of quicksilver. If any one, says the philosopher Aristotle, would coagulate quicksilver so as to change it into gold or the Stone, he must do so by means of sulphur, for whenever sulphur is withdrawn from the quicksilver it becomes liquid as before; unless, therefore, the sulphur remain permanently with the quicksilver, it cannot become gold or the Stone. Moreover, quicksilver is white, and the Stone is universally admitted to be red —hence sulphur must form part of its substance. Yet we answer as before, that quicksilver alone is the whole material cause, and the whole substance of the Stone.

You should, however, know that quicksilver in its first creation has many parts of an earthy, white, sulphureous matter mingled with it, which are most subtle and belong to its own material substance, and without which it would have no consistency. These particles cause first its white and then its red colour in the operation of the Magistery. Thus Aristotle calls quicksilver a water mingled with a certain subtle sulphureous earth. A hint to the same effect is thrown out by Geber in his chapter on the nature of quicksilver. There is an inward sulphur as well as an outward, he tells us, and this internal sulphur forms part of the substance of the quicksilver, and is the true agent in coagulating it. At least, both are not fixed, and both are instrumental in coagulating the Mercury. But when the quicksilver with its own inward sulphur is fixed and coagulated, and has received from it either the white or the red colour, then the external sulphur can no longer combine with it, because they have become dissimilar. Hence it may be urged that it cannot form part of the substance of our Stone.

Here we come upon the great secret of our Art, that quicksilver is coagulated, not by any mixture with anything else, but is both coagulated and coloured unto perfection by its own internal sulphur, while it is coloured and coagulated to corruption by external sulphur. If the quicksilver could be coagulated by any other substance, whether mineral, vegetable, or animal, it would be a foreign coagulum, and the coagulation would not be that which we require. We see, then, that this external sulphur, though it be active in metallic generation, cannot itself form part of the substance of our Stone; and the task before us is to get the quicksilver by itself, and to coagulate it without the contaminating influence of the outward sulphur, since that which generates cannot be part of the substance generated.

Chapter II.

Explains the Dictum of the Ancient Sages that "Sulphur alone is the matter of the Stone and of Gold."

THOSE who superficially skim the writings of the Sages might arrive at the conclusion that sulphur alone is the substance of our Stone. So Rosinus says that incombustible sulphur, which has prevailed against fire, is that which the Sages are in search of, and, elsewhere, that no tincture can be obtained except through pure water of sulphur. Again, the precious colour of the philosophers is derived from sulphur. So, also, Solomon, the son of David, calls sulphur the Stone which God has placed above all other stones, which is prized by those who know it, and thought vile by the multitude. Bulus, in the *Turba Philosophorum*, asserts that the pure water is obtained from sulphur, yet not from one sulphur only, but from several things which make up one sulphur. And Anaxagoras exclaims: " Know that the perfection of this work is the water of sulphur."

To this question we, nevertheless, answer, as above, that the perfection of our Magistery consists in quicksilver alone, which contains in its composition dry, sulphureous particles, which tinge and colour it white in actuality, and red in potentiality, and are that which gives to it perfection and form. But, as this internal sulphur cannot be active without some outward impulse, Nature has added to it, in all metallic ore, a certain external sulphur which stirs it into action. Our Magistery, of course, imitates Nature in this respect. Because of this inward sulphur, which coagulates the quicksilver, and forms part of it, and is unknown to the multitude, the ancient Sages have spoken of quicksilver as sulphur, and this hidden sulphur is made manifest in the Magistery of our Art by a grand artifice. Our sulphur, say they, is not the sulphur of the multitude, because common sulphur burns with a black smoke and is consumed; but the sulphur of the Sages burns with a white smoke and is perfected thereby. It is this sulphur which whitens and imparts the red colour, and coagulates and perfects the quicksilver into the substance of gold in Nature, and of the Philosopher's Stone in our Art.

It should be observed that, as everything is composed of matter and form, and is what it is by virtue of its form, a thing has the more being the more it possesses of the form. Quantity does not enter into the definition of form, since quantity and passivity belong to matter. When the substance is small in proportion to the form, there is much activity, much virtue, with great intensity of being, because there is proportionately much form. Concentrated force is more powerful than that which is divided. If this be so, we may say that, as the red luminous sulphur hidden in the quicksilver is the form of gold, it is that which tinges and transforms every kind of metal into gold. For this reason, the tincture is said to be derived rather from the quality and form, or sulphur, than from the quantity, or quicksilver. The intense redness thereof approaches black, or the colour of liver and of aloes, as declared in the *Book of Three Words*. Since one part of it tinges and forms a thousand parts of any metal into gold, according to the concensus of the philosophers, it must have much strength, a concentrated entity, and much form, or, rather, itself is the pure form of gold. Hence, on account of its redness, its operation can be extended to a great quantity of any kind of metal, so as to tinge and perfect it into gold. When the Stone is brought into loving contact with common metals, it purges away the external corrupting sulphur; thus they become white, and of the nature of pure quicksilver, and the form of gold being added to its substance, of course they become gold. This tincture, by means of which the perfecting process is brought about, is the sulphur of the Sages, the divine sulphur, and the Stone of the Philosophers, the secret sulphur with which all things are aureated and beautified. It is the precious substance which the Sages call by so many mysterious names: the Shadow of the Sun, the coagulum of quicksilver, that which flies with things flying and rests with things at rest, the gold of the Philosophers, that which is sought of many and found of few, the Quintessence, the salt of armonia, the Vinegar of the Sages, the Golden Tree, of whose fruit whosoever eats shall not hunger again; that which is nourished and generated in the fire, and delights in it as in its native element; that which, like man, is a microcosm or little world. It is the second sulphur which is joined to the first sulphur, producing a third sulphur, of which it is said that sulphurs are contained in sulphurs.

Note concerning the Water and the Oil of Sulphur.

The water of sulphur, or oil of

sulphur, is quicksilver extracted from this composite sulphur. It is a living water, and that which the sages call the Virgin's Milk, the pure, heavenly, and glorious water. It is sometimes referred to as the flying bird, which is substantially identical with the said sulphur, but diverse from the vulgar kind.

Is Sulphur alone the whole Material of Gold?

Some have said that gold is a substance which is digested in the bowels of the earth out of a most pure orange-coloured sulphur alone, with an admixture of quicksilver just sufficient to give it brightness and malleability. But they say that gold receives from sulphur its substance, colour, fusibility, and all the rest of its proper accidents. We answer that the ancient sages had some good reason for connecting each of the seven metals with one of the seven planets, as the heavenly influence from which it derived its peculiar properties. Thus, lead was assigned to Saturn, tin to Jupiter, iron to Mars, gold to the

Sun, copper to Venus, silver to the Moon. But to Mercury they assigned no metal, because only these six have attained to coagulation, with fusibility and malleability. In the seventh place, however, they did place Mercury, not as a metal, but as the First Matter of all metals. If they had thought that this place belonged to sulphur, they would have associated sulphur, and not Mercury, with the seventh planet. Hence, it must be concluded that quicksilver, and not sulphur, is the origin, matter, and substance of metals.

The question now arises as to what Aristotle meant by refusing to identify the material of a thing with its form, as was done by the Platonists and the Pythagoreans. It is clear from his words that he did not take the meaning of the ancient Sages. The material of Alchemy—the first matter, or chaos, according to the ancients, is that in which everything exists in a confused state, *i.e.*, the quicksilver of the Sages in its primary condition, generated by a kind of preliminary digestion. This is the Stone which they seek, concealed from the senses, but manifested to the mind, the form and flower of gold. The knowledge of this material is more important than anything else in Alchemy. For it opens up the knowledge of all other causes, properties, and conditions, and, finally, of the form itself. But if we do not know the right material, it is simply impossible for us to know anything about it. Hence, this question: What is the material?—must be the first problem solved by the student of Alchemy.

This material is, of course, by its very nature, disposed to receive its own proper form, just as the grain of wheat has in it the disposition to become wheat. Thus, if we define matter as that in which the form inheres, there is, after all, not so much difference between material and form, but that, in our Art at least, we may confidently identify them. There could be no such thing as a substantial form, if there were no material possessing a capacity of being developed in a certain direction. If anyone, then, would know the form of gold, he must first know the material of the Stone. Hence, we see that real insight into the nature of a thing depends on an accurate knowledge of its material.

Chapter III.

We must now proceed to enquire what are the Elements of the Stone, and how they are the same in gold as in all composite substances, not only on earth, but also in the heavens.

WE affirm that all elements of the Stone must be first purified, and then evenly mixed in the right proportions, so that the resultant compound may be permanent. Hence it is necessary to say something about the elements. There are many persons at the present day, even as there were some in the past, and will be others in the future, so long as investigators abide by the literal words of the Sages, who know not the meaning of our Art, and are endeavouring to extract the Philosopher's Stone from all sorts of fantastic animal and vegetable substances. These substances they have subjected to all the processes described in our orthodox treatises, and have obtained in the end something white, and something red, which, however, have none of the blessed properties of our Stone. These persons do not know that every form must be extracted from that proximate matter in which it is potentially contained; that is to say, the material and the form must both belong to the same natural genus. If we wish to understand the nature of a man, we shall not waste our time in studying the essential properties of a tree or of a stone; for then we should never get beyond these substances, which, however interesting in themselves, are quite foreign to our subject. Alchemy sets itself to transmute metals into gold; hence we must study the essential properties of gold and of the other metals, and we must look for our first substance among metals, and not in the animal or vegetable world. Know, then, that a knowledge of the essence and nature of a thing is obtained from a knowledge of its first principles, or proximate causes.

We cannot understand the changes of bodies, or even of quicksilver itself, if we have no radical knowledge of its essential properties. The principles of being and of knowing, says Aristotle, are the same—as things are, so they must also be understood and known. If we understand the substance of our Stone as it is, there is nothing left to study but the method of treatment, and this method will be suggested by the knowledge we already possess.

Every compound consists of a mixture of four elements, two of which are enclosed, viz., fire and air, while two enclose them, viz., earth and water, whence we see that in every composite there is a superabundance of earth and water. Fire and air are the formal and moving principles, the two others are the material and passive principles. The virtue of fire and air can appear only in earth and water, as the virtue of the form can appear only in the substance. For even as the form is included or hidden in the matter, so are fire and air concealed in earth and water. Rhasis calls fire and air the occult, water and earth the manifest, principles of a compound. Since, then, the strong are enclosed by the weak, the compound is easily corrupted, and the formal principles by their exhalation give to the others form, colour, taste, smell, etc.; but so long as the material principles remain, they are not wholly deserted by the formal. If, on the other hand, the compound is not easily destroyed, it is on account of the strength of the enclosing principles. If both are weak, the whole compound is very perishable, *e.g.*, camphor. If both are equally strong, every smallest part of the compound coheres in a permanent union with every other. When the humid and the dry, and the hot and the cold, are so evenly balanced that there is an equilibrium of the elements, they are perfectly united, and the compound is indestructible.

The elements of our Art, then, are the humid and the dry, *i.e.*, water and earth. In water there is enclosed air, and in earth fire. But the radical element from which all others are derived, is humidity, or water, that is, liquefaction, or, according to others, earth. We may reconcile the two views by stating, on the authority of Empedocles, that when water is thickened, it becomes earth: earth floats upon the waters, and is founded upon the waters, as we learn from Morienus and Hermes. When wax is in a liquid state, it is like water; when it becomes coagulated, it is dry, like earth; and yet its weight is the same in both cases. Alexander sets forth, in his *Epistle*, that all the Philosophers apply the name of fire to everything that is hot, of water to all that is fluxible, and of earth or stone to whatsoever is coagulated. But neither water nor any other element by itself is of much use to us in this Art. They must all be first separated and severally purified, and then recombined in even proportions—that is to say, when the water has been purified, we must add to it the purified earth, and then we shall have all the four indissolubly united, and the work will be perfect. If they are not so united, the fire resolves the water into steam, together with the earth, and the whole compound perishes. If, then, you would succeed in mixing elements, you must know their nature and properties. Convert the elements, says Alexander; make the humid dry, and the volatile fixed, and you have what you seek. Know that, then, all elements are actually converted into earth, and the other elements are, and remain, with it potentially and virtually. Hence, Hermes says that earth is the element out of which everything is made, and into which everything is converted. In the composition of the Stone and of gold we have a perfect equation of the elements. This well-tempered substance can neither be destroyed by the violence of the fire, nor vitiated by the impurity of the earth, nor spoiled by an excess of water or air. The Stone and gold are thus generated in the fire, and, like everything else, flourish in their native element. They are, therefore, indestructible by fire, and are rather perfected and improved by it than otherwise.

These remarks, in the opinion of the ancient Sages, had a direct bearing upon the constitution of the heavenly bodies. They, like the Philosopher's Stone, are composed of such an evenly balanced mixture of the elements as to be indestructible The active and passive elements are so accurately matched in their composition that the formal cannot be separated from the material principles. Hence, Nature has placed nearest to them the sphere of fire, which conserves rather than destroys them. For elementary fire is related to the heavenly bodies as material fire is related to gold and our Stone. It is through this wise natural arrangement that the heavenly bodies may be said to be practically indestructible and eternal.

There are, then, four elements, by reason of the four primary qualities; and they are mutually convertible, because every one is potentially in every other, and they are constantly generating and destroying each other. In substance, there is from the beginning of the world only one element, or First Matter, out of the conflicting qualities of which the four elements are generated by division. Similarly, there are in the first substance of this Stone four elements potentially, which by our Art are separated, and then again combined. Moreover, we believe our Stone to be incorruptible, not only through the equation of its elements, but also through the addition to it of the fifth element, just as the great world is composed of four corruptible elements, and an incorruptible one, which is the quintessence. It is this quintessence which, in the small world of our Art, holds the four elements together in indissoluble union, which also, according to Alexander, is neither hot nor cold, neither moist nor dry. This soul of our Art is the divine incorruptible sulphur. Other elements are the body, soul, and spirit, the dry and the humid, the fixed and the volatile, the white and the red. As of all elements earth alone is fixed, and as the elements at the end of our Magistery must become fixed, it is clear that they must all be converted into earth, or the fixed state of the philosophers.

Chapter IV.

Of the Ferment, and the modes, conditions, properties, and conversion brought about by it.

OF the ferment, which is the great secret of our Art, and without which it cannot attain its goal, the Sages speak only in the very obscurest terms. They seem to use the word in two senses, meaning either the elements of the Stone itself, or that which perfects and completes the Stone. In the first sense our Stone is the leaven of all other metals, and changes them into its own nature—a small piece of leaven leavening a whole lump. As leaven, though of the same nature with dough, cannot raise it, until, from being dough, it has received a new quality which it did not possess before, so our Stone cannot change metals, until it is changed itself, and has added to it a certain virtue which it did not possess before. It cannot change, or colour, unless it have first itself been changed and coloured, as we learn from the *Turba Philosophorum*. Ordinary leaven receives its fermenting power through the digestive virtue of gentle and hidden heat; and so our Stone is rendered capable of fermenting, converting, and altering metals by means of a certain digestive heat, which brings out its potential and latent properties, seeing that without heat, as Theophilus tells us, neither digestion, operation, nor motion are possible. The difference between ordinary leaven and our ferment is that common leaven loses nothing of its substance in the digestive process, while digestion removes from our ferment all that is superfluous, impure, and corruptive, as is done by Nature in the preparation of gold. It is because our ferment assimilates all metals to itself, just as common leaven assimilates to itself the whole mass of dough, that it has received this name from the Sages. Hence it appears that quicksilver (being of the same substance with the metals), when fermented and changed into the same substance as the ferment, transmutes into its own nature every fusible substance of its own kind, and, as its nature is that of gold, it converts all metals into gold.

It is true the action of this ferment is not quite analogous to that of leaven. For leaven changes the whole lump of dough into a kind of leaven; but our Stone, instead of converting metals into the Tincture, transmutes them only into gold. Our Stone rather changes all metals into a kind of intermediate substance, such as is the substance of gold, between that which they were before and the alterative ferment. The colour, too, of gold is intermediate between the blackness of iron, the redness of copper, the livid grey of lead, and the whiteness of silver. The degree of digestion which is obtained is also intermediate between that of copper and iron on the one hand, and that of tin and lead on the other. Its fusibility further represents the golden mean, since copper is melted with difficulty, iron with more difficulty, while tin and lead are melted with the greatest ease, and silver and gold not so readily as the latter, but more readily than the former. The same intermediate quality of gold is noticeable also in its ring, that of lead and tin being dull, while that of iron and copper is sharp, and that of silver and gold moderately clear. To this middle state all metals are reduced by our Stone. For, though the virtue of our Stone is great, yet, on being mixed with common metals, its action is slightly affected by their impurity, and does not change them quite into its own likeness, but only into gold.

More difficult is the second sense of the ferment, which is the truly philosophical ferment, and wherein is the whole difficulty of our Art, for in this second sense it signifies that which perfects our Stone. The word ferment is derived from a root which denotes seething or bubbling, because it makes the dough rise and swell, and has a hidden dominant quality which prevails to change the dough into its own nature, rectifying and reducing it to a better and nobler state. It is composed of divers hidden virtues inherent in one substance. In the same way that ferment which is mixed with our quicksilver makes it swell and rise, and prevails to assimilate it to its own nature, thus exalting it into a nobler condition. In itself quicksilver has no active virtue, but if it be mortified together with this ferment it remains joined to it for ever, and is thenceforward changed into the nature of the Sun, the whole being developed into ferment, which in turn develops all things into gold.

The ferment of which we speak is invisible to the eye, but capable of being apprehended by the mind. It is the body which retains the soul, and the soul can shew its power only when it is united to the body. Therefore, when the Artist sees the white soul arise, he should join it to its body in the very same instant; for no soul can be retained without its body. This union takes place through the mediation of the spirit, for the soul cannot abide in the body except through the spirit, which gives permanence to their union, and this conjunction is the end of the work. Now, the body is nothing new or foreign; only that which was before hidden becomes manifest, and *vice versa*. The body is stronger than soul and spirit, and if we are to retain them, we must do so by means of the body, as the *Turba* and Plato agree. Without this hidden spiritual body the Stone can neither ferment nor be perfected. Of course, the body, soul, and spirit of our Stone are only different aspects of the same thing, and according to these aspects the Sages call it now by one name, and now by another. The soul, says Plato, must be reunited to its own body, or else you will fail, because the soul will escape you. And Hermes insists that it must be its own original body, and not one of an extraneous or alien nature, as attempted by some who are ignorant of this arcanum. Rhasis says that the body is the form, and the spirit the matter; and rightly, because as no substance can exist without form, which is its real being, so the soul, through the mediation of the spirit, cannot be in the Stone except by the body, because its being and perfection depend on the body. Hence, the body is their bond and form, though they are the same thing. As that which imparts its form to the Stone and to gold, is something fixed, and a body, while Mercury is that which receives fixation and a form, it follows that the body is the form.

The body, then, is that which is the form, and the ferment, and the perfection, and the Tincture of which the Sages are in search. It is also the Sol and gold of the philosophers. It is white actually and red potentially; while it is white it is still imperfect, but it is perfected when it becomes red. The Sun, says Rosinus, is white in appearance, and red by development. Anaxagoras teaches that the Sun is an ardent red, but the soul to which the Sun is united by the bond of the spirit is white, being of the nature of the Moon, and is called the quicksilver of the philosophers. Hermes tells us that without the Red Stone there can be no true Tincture. The red slave, says Rhasis, has wedded a white spouse. We now see the truth of the saying that there are two kinds of gold, one white and one red; but the one must be in the other. This white gold is, according to Rhasis, a neutral body, which is neither in sickness nor in health, and it is, of course, quicksilver. Geber say that no metal is submerged in it except gold, which is the medium of conjunction between the tinctures. That it is the true ferment, Hermes tells us in his seventh book, when he says: Note, that the ferment whitens the compound, prevents combustion, holds the tincture together, preserves bodies from evaporating, and makes them enter each other and remain in union, etc. So also Morienus affirms that the ferment of gold is gold, as the ferment of dough is dough.

From these considerations we see clearly how silver and gold are of the same nature, and that silver precedes gold, and is predisposed to gold, while gold is hidden in silver, and is extracted from its womb. Hence, Senior says that the rising sun is in the waxing moon. Know, ye students of this Art, cries Zeno in the *Turba Philosophorum*, that unless you first make it white, you will not be able to make it red, because the white potentially contains the red. If there be too little gold in the compound, says Dardanus, the Tincture will be brilliantly white. Alphidius says: Know that the dealbation must come first, for it is the beginning of the whole work, and then the rubefaction must follow, which is the perfection of the whole work. Since the entire substance, viz., the soul united to the body by the spirit, is of the pure nature of gold, it is clear that whatever it converts, it must convert into gold. At first, indeed, the whole mass is white, because quicksilver predominates; but because gold is dominant, though hidden, in it, when it is ferment, the mass in the second stage of our Magistery becomes red in the fulness of the potential sense, while in the third stage, or the second and last decoction, the ferment is actively dominated, and the red colour becomes manifest, and possesses the whole substance. Again, we say that this ferment is that strong substance which turns everything into its own nature. Our ferment is of the same substance as gold; gold is of quicksilver, and our design is to produce gold.

The Ancients gave the name of body to whatsoever is fixed and resists the action of heat; moreover, it has the power of retaining in a compound that which is essentially incorporeal and volatile, and attempts to volatilize the body, viz., the soul. Spirit they called that which constitutes the bond between body and soul, and, by abiding with the body, compels the soul to return to it. And yet body, soul, and spirit are not three things, but different aspects of the same thing. As bond between body and soul, the spirit is said to prevail during the Magistery from beginning to end; so long as the substance is volatile and flees from the fire, it is called soul; when it becomes able to resist the action of the fire, it is called body. The force of the body should prevail over the force of the soul, and instead of the body being carried upward with the soul, the soul remains with the body, the work is crowned with success, and the spirit will abide with the two in indissoluble union for ever. Since, then, the body perfects and retains the soul, and imparts real being to it and the whole work, while the soul manifests its power in this body, and all this is accomplished through the mediation of the spirit, it has been well said that the body and the form are one and the same thing, the other two being called the substance.

But how are we to understand

Plato's remark that he who has once performed this work need not repeat it, as his fortune is made for ever? The words do not mean that he who has once prepared the Tincture can multiply its quantity indefinitely, just as he who has once struck fire out of a stone can always keep himself provided with fire simply by adding fuel to it. The authority of Plato is supported by that of Rhasis, who speaks in a similar fashion. They should be interpreted, however, not according to the letter, but according to the spirit. He who has once succeeded in preparing this Medicine need not any more go through the experience of all his failures and mistakes: he now knows how to perform all the processes of our Magistery properly, and, therefore, if ever he should need a fresh supply of the Medicine, he will be able to provide himself with it without much trouble.

When the Alchemist, in the course of his decoction and putrefaction, has reached the end of the first part of our

Magistery, in which is seen the simple white colour, before the appearance of any other colours, then he must straightway set about the second part of the work, and this second part is the ferment and the fermentation of the substance. Then, if all elements are evenly combined without being touched by hand, the artist is a rich man, and has no need thenceforth, in repeating the work, to repeat all his former mistakes. But, if he does not combine the elements evenly, the whole substance will vanish into thin air, and the Alchemist will have lost his hoped-for riches. If, says Haly, you do not find this Stone, when it germinates, no other will arise in its place. Beware, says Plato, lest in the fermentation you come to a bitter end. If there be any hindrance or obstacle in the solution, there will most likely be corruption in the augmenting. The right moment must be seized here, as in all other things. When you are baking bread or sweetmeats, or any other solid substance, the moment will arrive when they are perfectly done; and if after that moment you leave them in the oven ever so short a time, they will be marred, burnt, and destroyed. Haly compares the preparation of our Stone to that of soap, which is spoiled if boiled beyond a certain point. Hence the artist must be extremely watchful, and as soon as the substance has reached its most subtle stage, he must put an end to the digestive process; if he pushes it any further, the combined forces of the fire and the volatile part of the substance overcome its fixed part, and the whole evaporates. He who knows how to pacify and assuage the hostility of the elements will be successful in our Magistery, but no other.

The object of what has been said is to shew that at the close of the perfect decoction and putrefaction, Nature, by the ministration of our Art, generates a bare simple matter, not united to its form; this matter the Ancients called first matter, on account of its resemblance to the first matter of the world, before it received its form. This matter needs to be united to its form, which form is the ferment, and is hidden in its womb. This conjunction must take place immediately the matter is born; the same will then become durable and imperishable. Nature, unassisted, cannot effect this union, because it is irrational, and its operations go on for ever in successive renovation and destruction; but the Artist can watch the proper moment, and preserve that which the fire has generated. Now, when the conjunction has taken place, the substance has nothing more to fear from the fire. If one only knows the right moment, the conjunction is a very easy process; and when it takes place, there are many wonderful phenomena, as Morienus testifies. It is brought about by a well-tempered fire, the action of which is stopped in time by a watchful artist. And this conjunction accomplished, it is open to the artist to rest. Socrates, in the *Turba Philosophorum*, says that what follows is woman's work and child's play. Rhasis says that nothing but vigilance is requisite, for as the ablution and depuration of the elements are accomplished by the presence of fire, so are the conjunction, perpetuation, and fermentation of the purified matters performed in the absence of fire.

Concerning the Time of Fermentation.

It should further be noticed that the time for fermenting the substance is the moment when the Stone germinates, germination being the revival of a seed after apparent death. The quicksilver first melts through the digestive action of the fire, and is then coagulated with its ferment or body: this process is that which we call germination. What a man sows, says Rhasis, that shall he also reap. Seeds can only spring up after their kind, and bear fruit after their kind. So minerals do not become something else, but return to that from which they arose.

Yet, how can Nature generate a simple substance not united to its form? This is, nevertheless, a fact according to the ancients, but in a metaphorical sense. Aristotle says that as the reason comes to man from without, so the vegetative and sensitive soul comes from within. There is in seed the soul and the body, but there is added to it from without the rational spirit. In the same way we are to understand the metaphorical dicta in our Art.

Again, the action of heat in itself is not determined in any particular direction, or towards any particular end; but for the attainment of any such purpose it has to be used and regulated by an intelligent mind. When I say heat, I mean the elementary fire which is generated in all things, both animals, and vegetables, and metals. This natural fire, without which there is neither growth nor generation, is the instrument of the mind, and is regulated by the Artist, in respect of quantity, quality, and time, for the attainment of a certain well-defined end. If the heat be continued beyond a certain point, the form which it had generated is again destroyed. The action of fire in itself only tends to combustion, but man may regulate it so as to effect many other objects. Hence, Pythagoras says that man is the measure of all things. Nature is blind and its action indefinite; it follows all the influences which are brought to bear on it, in this or in that direction; but the will of man is free, and can regulate and modify the working of Nature so as to bring about its own ends. If the will of man follow Nature, Nature will go beyond the proper point, and spoil everything.

The object of Nature in all things is to introduce into each substance the form which properly belongs to it; and this is also the design of our Art. When, therefore, the quicksilver of the Sages has been generated by the skill and wisdom of the artist, the form must be added to it, and then the work stopped at once, since its end is reached, and anything more can only spoil it.

If the Mercury were coagulated by some foreign (non-metallic) substance, it would not be of the slightest use, since in Nature only homogeneous things will combine. The coagulation by means of arsenic and common sulphur, though they are mineral substances, tends only to corruption.

Chapter V.

What is theriac, and what is called the poison in the Philosopher's Stone?

THE Ancients have mentioned, as component parts of this Stone, theriac and poison. Like the ferment, they are either the perfect Stone, or that which perfects it. In the first sense it is improperly, in the second more properly, so called. Because theriac has remarkable cleansing properties, and poison possesses considerable medicinal virtues, they may mean the Stone, which cleanses common metals from all impurities, and converts them into gold. The four corrupt metals suffer from four different kinds of leprosy, and, therefore, each needs this poison for its cure. Iron is affected with leprosy from corruption of the bile, copper from corruption of the blood, tin from corruption of the phlegm, and lead from simple melancholic corruption, which is also called elephantiasis. All these corruptions are due to the presence of impure sulphur, which is removed by our poison, or washed away by means of our theriac. Silver suffers from a phlegmatic leprosy, because it contains a proportion of combustible sulphur. But wise Nature in the generation thereof has combined a certain theriac therein, and when the sulphur has been purged off by the Stone, gold immediately results. Gold alone is free from impurity and is perfectly healthy, like pure blood in a sound body. In its correct sense, theriac or poison is that which is properly termed ferment. If the Artist stops at the right moment, all will be well; otherwise, the process of fermentation will go too far, and everything will be spoiled. Hence Hamec says that at this stage the ferment may become poison, and the Artist must very carefully beware of its smell, for, if he inhale it, it will prove fatal to him. He means to say that if it be allowed to evaporate, the Artist will be ruined. This Stone, says Morienus, heals the infirmities of metals, as theriac cures the diseases of the human body; hence it is sometimes called poison, on account of its medicinal use.

Note.—Of the union of Soul and Body with their Spirit.

At the close of our Magistery, when the soul seeks its body, we should see that it is able to unite itself to it, and receive life and activity. This union and composition take place through the operation of the spirit. When the soul is united to the body, it lives with its body for ever. The conjunction occurs at the moment of the soul's resurrection: for, though it existed before, yet it could not manifest itself in the body, on account of the defilement and impurity of the body. Hence it lay like a thing dead and useless, and, as it were, buried with its body. But when it is purified and made white by means of our Magistery, it rises clean and white, and finds the body from which it had been separated also clean and pure, and so it seeks its body, and longs to be united to it, in order that it may live for ever: for it cannot be united to a strange body. If, therefore, the Artist does not take care, it will seek to escape with its body, and carry it upward, when the whole work will be annihilated, and the end of the experiment made void. Hence the body is called the theriac of its soul when the soul is saved by it and is beatified with it; it is called poison when it is the cause of the eternal death of the soul, through a failure in conjunction by reason of the Artist's folly. But if he seizes the right moment to stop the heat, the union is perfected and is rendered indissoluble. In this conjunction the body is spiritual, like the soul itself. Thus they unite, as water unites with water, and body, soul, and spirit are now the same thing, nor can they be separated for ever. Because of the insight which their Art gave to them, the Ancient Sages knew all about the resurrection of the body and the redeeming work of Jesus Christ, as also about the Trinity in Unity, and all the other verities of our faith. I am firmly persuaded that any unbeliever who got truly to know this Art, would straightway confess the truth of our Blessed Religion, and believe in the Trinity and in our Lord Jesus Christ. Such was the experience of Hermes, Plato, and other ancient Sages.

But we will now return to the point. We were speaking of theriac and poison. When this Stone is born in the coction, it is in the likeness of brilliantly white quicksilver, and is called the quicksilver of the Sages. This quicksilver, to be of any utility, must be joined to its body and mortified; it is killed by its body, and therefore the body may be called poison, in the second and proper sense. And as this death tends to healing and glorious restoration, it is, in the same way, designated theriac. So it is with men: death is the means of giving to them a more glorious life. Our poison, or theriac, is thus identical with the above-mentioned ferment, and is the key of the whole work, the form of the Sun, and the flower of gold. Hence it is advanced by Zeno, in the *Turba Philosophorum*, that no body is more precious and pure than the Sun, and that no tinging poison can be generated without the Sun and its shadow; whoever thinks otherwise errs grievously, but he who tinges the poison of the Wise by the Sun and its shadow, the same attains unto the great arcanum. Without this theriac and poison our Magistery cannot be accomplished; though, of course, they are not added from without, but form an integral part of our substance.

Chapter VI.

The Coagulum and the Milk in the Philosopher's Stone, and its male and female agents.

THE terms used in the superscription are some of the most secret phrases of our Art, and if we do not know their meaning, we know nothing about Alchemy. Some suppose that this Stone, when perfect, is related to Mercury, as a coagulating substance to milk. For, as a moderate quantity of a coagulum clots a large quantity of milk, so a small particle of this Stone, when projected upon many parts of Mercury, converts them into silver or gold. This view, however, is a great mistake. If it were true, of what use would the Stone be for the conversion of metals which are already coagulated by Nature? We say that the coagulum of the Sages is that which, in the preceding chapters, has been called the ferment, or the body, or the poison, or the flower of gold, which is hidden in the Mercury of the Sages when it arises, and that Mercury is called the Milk. The coagulum is that which coagulates the Mercury, and the two are one and the same in substance, *i.e*, Mercury coagulates itself, and is not coagulated by any foreign substance, as you may also see in the case of wax when it is coagulated. Moreover, as coagulum is made of milk alone, but receives the power of coagulation by means of a certain digestion and decoction, so this coagulum which arises in the Mercury of the Philosophers by means of certain digestion and decoction, receives power to coagulate the Mercury in which it is; and as the coagulum changes a large quantity of milk into its own nature, so it is with the coagulum of Mercury and its substance. Mercury, thus coagulated, is no longer volatile, but has become the gold of the Sages, and their poison.

Know that this coagulum is the Key of the Sages, because when it coagulates the spirit, it at the same time dissolves the body, the coagulation of the spirit and the solution of the body thus being the same thing, whence the philosophers have laid down that the spirits cannot be detained except with the waters of their bodies. Our gum coagulates our milk, says Rhasis, and our milk dissolves our gum, after which appears the morning redness. When I saw water coagulate itself, says Senior, I was sure that all I had been told was true; this coagulated water they call the male, and they espouse it to a female, whose son he is, and is also his root and coagulation. Female they call the milk which is coagulated, and male that which coagulates; for activity belongs to the male, and passivity to the female. The first is the fixed part of quicksilver, and the second its liquid and volatile part—out of their mixture arises the Stone. The male and the female, being joined together, become one body. Venerate, says Alexander, the king and his queen, and do not burn them. The male is under the female, and has no wings; the female has wings, and desires to fly, but the male holds her back. Hence the philosophers say: make the woman rise over the man, and the man rise over the woman. So also Rosinus: The woman is fortified by the man.

I must repeat that the male and the female are the same in the same subject, and yet have different and even contrary qualities. It is like the male and female principles in any vegetable seed, or the active and the passive principle in an egg. Thus, when the Stone first comes into existence, it has in it a mixture of the male and female principles, but at first it is liquid, fluent, volatile, bright, and capable of coagulation, *i.e.*, female. The coagulum in its womb is solid, permanent, fixed, and produces coagulation in the other, *i.e.*, is male. The female that flees is passive, white, and easily caught by the male; the male that pursues is red, and seizes and holds the female with great strength.

Similarly, the Sages have compared the two principles in our substance to an old and a young man, because the colour of old age is white, while that of youth is ruddy and bright. Hence Rhasis: The stone of our science in the beginning is an ancient and in the end a boy, because it is first white and afterwards red.

They have also given geographical names to this substance, calling the humid principle the Egyptian, and the dry principle the Persian; Egypt the house of humidity, and Persia the house of dryness. The Egyptians, says Melvescindus, need the help of the Persians. All putrefaction takes place in humid substances, but the end of putrefaction is dryness and incineration. The putrefaction begins in Egypt, but its end is in Persia. They have also described our substance by saying that the white female has the red male in her womb, and is in the travail throes. The coagulation will then be the accomplishment of the birth; that which was within now coming out, and that which is fluxible becoming fixed. Such are a few metaphors under which our substance has been described.

Chapter VII.

This is a chapter of the different similitudes of the Generation and Birth of the Embryo out of the Menstrual Blood, and of a chicken out of an egg—considered as analogous to the Birth of Gold out of Sulphur and Quicksilver.

WE will now proceed to illustrate our meaning still further by the help of some analogies. The first analogy we shall select is the generation of the fœtus in the mother's womb. The generation of the fœtus is brought about by the male sperm, in conjunction with the female menstrual blood. The latter is the substance, the former the active principle. As soon as the form is generated, the sperm is purged off. In generation, the male contributes the form and the active principle, the female contributes the substance and the body. The sperm is to the menstrual blood what the carpenter is to the wood in producing a bench, hence the sperm is not part of the thing generated. So gold is caused by sulphur as the efficient or active means and by quicksilver as the substantial or passive means. And as the sperm informs with a form similar to itself, and not foreign, so is it in like manner with sulphur. The outward sulphur acts by digestion upon the inward sulphur which is latent in the quicksilver, and causes it to inform, coagulate, colour, and fix the quicksilver into the form of gold or of the Stone of the Philosophers.

It should also be observed that the sperm generates out of the substance first the heart, thus impressing upon the heart the generative virtue which belongs to it as part of the living body. Then the sperm is separated from the heart, because now the heart is able of itself to form the other members by means of the generative power imparted to it by the sperm. When the sperm has generated the heart, its work is done, and all that remains is performed by the heart. The same principle holds good in the germination of plants. When the seed, in which all the generative force is at first inherent, has sent forth the germ or shoot, the seed itself withers and decays, as something which has henceforth become useless, and the power of generating the rest of the plant is now inherent in the germ or shoot. When the germ has once been formed, it no longer needs the seed, but produces leaves, flowers, and seed out of itself. Thus the germ is, like the heart, generated and then separated from its sperm.

In the same way, we declare that the outward sulphur generates out of the quicksilver a certain sulphur which is like the heart, and to which henceforth belongs all the generative force of the outward sulphur. Thus, the outward sulphur, being no longer needed, is purged off. The sperm, which in our case is the sulphur, having introduced the form into the quicksilver, by means of the internal sulphur, having done its work, is no longer wanted.

You should know that since it is unnecessary for the moving principle continually to keep in contact with that which it moves, provided it has once touched it, as you may see from the case of the archer and the arrow, so the sperm, and the heart generated by the sperm, need not always keep up their connection. In the same way, as soon as the outward sulphur has touched the quicksilver, and generated or created another sulphur out of the quicksilver, which now possesses the power of generating and imparting the form of gold, it is not necessary that the outward sulphur should remain any longer in contact with the quicksilver; it is sufficient that it has touched it in the past. Hence it is fitting that what is extrinsic should be separated, as something corruptible from what is incorruptible.

Again, in human generation, if the sperm be sufficiently powerful, and has sufficient heat to assimilate the whole of the menstrual blood to itself, the sperm, coming as it does from a male, will naturally produce a male in the mother's womb. But if the sperm have not sufficient heat or strength, it will not be able to digest the female substance; the latter will, therefore, prevail, and a female will be the result. The consequence of this arrangement is that females have not so much natural heat as males. It is the same with our sulphur and quicksilver. If the inward sulphur has sufficient heat to digest the whole of the quicksilver, it assimilates the quicksilver to itself, and the whole is changed into gold. In the contrary case, the quicksilver will prevail and change the whole substance into silver. Hence gold is yellow like sulphur, and silver is white like mercury. But the yellowness and whiteness in quicksilver are not of double origin; both are of the quicksilver, just as the white and yellow of an egg are both the product of the female bird. In other metals, the sulphur has not yet been able to digest the quicksilver because of its want of heat, as in lead and tin, or it has burnt the quicksilver by means of its excessive heat, as in iron and copper.

For the heat of the sulphur may be in excess as well as too little, and thus digestion may be prevented in two opposite ways. When heat is too great it dries up the humidity of the substance, and when it is too small it is choked by this humidity. Too much fire will spoil the food, and too little will not be sufficient to cook it. Gold alone, of all the metals, is properly digested by temperate heat, and silver in the same way; but all other metals suffer either from excess or defect of heat.

But, after all, we should remember, with Aristotle, that the real motive principle in sperm is not the sperm itself, but the soul of the person who generates with the sperm, as with an instrument. It is the soul of the workman which uses his arm as an instrument to shape the timber or to fashion the sword. The intelligent soul of man, through the medium of the spirit or blood, moves the hand as an instrument, and the hand moves the outward substance. So the soul of the person generating uses the seed or sperm as an instrument, and acts on the substance or menstrual blood indirectly through the sperm. It is the same with sulphur and quicksilver in the generation of metals; sulphur is not the principal agent, but the occult mineral virtue, or chief intrinsic agent, which acts with the heavenly bodies, and makes an instrumental use of the sulphur; which, then, in its turn, moves the quicksilver, as a substance proper for the generation to which it is moved by the first agents. In this Art, the soul or intelligence of the Artist, wherein are the species and the knowledge, is the real, extrinsic, moving cause, and imparts its purpose to the digestive and liquefactive mineral virtue, which again, in its turn, moves directly the outward sulphur, and indirectly the inward sulphur and the quicksilver. Liquefaction, coagulation, and other accidents, are brought about by cold and heat, but the form is produced by the movement of instrumental forces which are themselves set in motion by the intelligent mind of the Artist, who modifies, tempers, and aids the action of natural conditions.

The Analogy of Common Quicksilver.

As the egg of the hen without the seed of the male bird can never become a chicken, so common quicksilver without sulphur can never become gold, or the Stone of the Philosophers, because without sulphur it has no generative virtue; again, sulphur without quicksilver can never become gold, or the Stone, because it is like the seed and sperm of the male, and there is no generation without the menstrual blood of the female, which is the substance and nutriment of generation. The generation of gold is of quicksilver, and its nutriment (like that of the chicken in the egg) is of the yellow substance, namely, sulphur. Hence the Stone is generated of the white, *i.e.*, quicksilver, and the nutriment of the yellow, *i.e.*, its hidden sulphur digested by the action of the outward sulphur through the regulative power of our Art. Nature has wisely mingled the sulphur and common quicksilver, the male and the female substance, in metals, for the purpose of their generation. And as everything attains to growth and development by the same principles to which it owes its generation, so gold and the Stone must be perfected by the action of homogeneous substances, and not by substances foreign to them. So, also, if imperfect metals are to be changed into gold by means of the Stone, even this agent can make use only of that substance in them which is identical with that of gold, while all foreign corruptive elements must be purged off; this means that only out of quicksilver can gold be generated by the mediation of the Stone, for which reason the sulphurous elements which are in the common metals are heterogeneous, and must be removed, because they will not amalgamate with it. Those, again, who attempt to prepare our Stone out of non-metallic substances are grievously at fault, and spend their labour in vain.

The artist who would prepare the Stone, must take for his substance neither common quicksilver alone, nor common sulphur alone, nor yet a mixture of common quicksilver and common sulphur, but a substance in which Nature herself, who is the handmaid of Art, has combined quicksilver and sulphur. The two substances of which we speak are really one substance, and are never found apart. They are capable of developing into gold, and this development actually takes place under favourable circumstances. For as we see that geographical situation has an influence in either elevating or degrading animal and vegetable forms, we may conclude that the same probably holds good in the case of metals. Local influences may sometimes be favourable to the development of sulphur and quicksilver into gold, or they may cause the process of development to stop short at one of the imperfect metals. Again, the imperfection of the common metals may be owing to a corrupt state of the surrounding earth, or to an excess of bad sulphur.

Chapter VIII.

Refutation of some objections. It is said that copper and iron cannot become gold and silver. How this is possible. The difficulty solved.

MANY admit that those common metals which are still in a crude and half-digested state can have their digestion completed so as to become gold. But, they say it is different with iron and copper, which, through the excessive quality of their digestive heat, have already passed the proper point of temperate digestion, and, therefore, can never be brought back to the intermediate state indicated by gold. Food which is insufficiently cooked, may be cooked till it is done; but there is no means of restoring food which has been burnt to a right condition.

It should, however, be observed that there are in all varieties of metal, except gold, two kinds of sulphur, one external and scorching, the other inward and non-combustive, being of the substantial composition of quicksilver. The outward sulphur is separable from them; the inward sulphur is not. The outward sulphur, then, is not, in any real sense, united to the quicksilver: hence the quicksilver cannot be really scorched by it. If this be so, it follows that when the quicksilver is purified by the removal of the outward sulphur, it is restored to its original condition, and can be transmuted into gold and silver, whether it be found in tin and lead, or in iron and copper; and we may justly conclude from these considerations that when the Philosophers' Stone is projected upon iron or copper in a liquefied state, it mingles in a moment of time with all the particles of quicksilver existing in them, and with these only, as they alone are of a nature homogeneous with its own, and perfects them into the purest gold, while all particles of external sulphur are purged off, because they are not of a nature homogeneous with that of the Philosophers' Stone. For quicksilver always most readily combines with any substance that is of the same nature with itself, and rejects and casts out everything heterogeneous. It does not matter what are the other constituent parts of a metal; if it be a metal, and contain quicksilver, that quicksilver can be changed into gold by means of the Philosophers' Stone. So we see that, in the case of milk, the coagulum clots only those parts of the milk which are of a nature homogeneous with its own. The scorching to which our objectors refer, has taken place only in the sulphur of iron and copper; the quicksilver is not at all affected by this adverse influence, as any experimental chemist will tell you. If we burn or coagulate quicksilver with sulphur, and make from their sublimation what is called uzifur (that is, cinnabar from sulphur and mercury), after the magistery of sublimation, we may separate the substance of the quicksilver from the uzifur, pure and clean, which shews that the quicksilver did not undergo combustion, but the sulphur only. It is the same in the cases of iron and copper, and in this manner the difficulty is settled.

This is the end of our Golden Investigation, extracted from the works of Bonus of Ferrara by Janus Therapus Lacinius, the Calabrian Minorite friar.

We hereunto append a letter written by Bonus to a friend with reference to this Magistery, which may serve to throw still further light upon the subject of our investigation.

HERE FOLLOWS THE EPISTLE OF BONUS OF FERRARA, A LEARNED DOCTOR OF MEDICINE AND OF THIS ART, TO ONE OF HIS FRIENDS.

YOU ask me to tell you the matter of the Stone which so many Sages have sought. Of course, any one who does not know this matter himself cannot impart the secret to others. But I have good reason to think that I know something about it; and I may speak to you out of the fulness of an experience gained through many bitter disappointments and failures. Nor do I think it sufficient to make a statement; I also desire to furnish you with the grounds of my belief. I will now reveal to you all that I have said at great length in the *New Pearl of Great Price* and in my *Tract against those who are at work upon a wrong matter*, addressed to Brother Anselm the Monk, in a private and confidential manner; and may God help me to speak clearly and in accordance with the truth of our Art!

You do not enquire after our method of procedure, which is the arcanum and glory of the whole world, as the philosophers testify, but you desire to have the matter of our Art made known to you; and this knowledge is in itself an inestimable boon to a beginner.

Know, then, that our arsenic or auripigment is composed by Nature of sulphur and quicksilver, as it is found in its original natural state. When arsenic is sublimed, it often happens that there comes out of it quicksilver in small globules like grains of millet, as every experimental chemist will tell you. This quicksilver is identical with ordinary quicksilver, which may be seen from the fact that it alone of all metallic substances will mingle with quicksilver, while the quicksilver retains all its own peculiar properties and qualities. Hence we conclude that in the composition of arsenic there is quicksilver. In the same way, we call sulphur the tincture of redness properly and by virtue of its own nature; quicksilver is the white tincture, as all Sages tell us. But if we project arsenic or realgar upon liquid copper, it will tinge that metal with a white colour like the whiteness of the Moon; this colour shews the presence of quicksilver. In all properly purified metals we find the nature of coagulated quicksilver rather than of sulphur; for sulphur exists in quicksilver in an occult manner.

Common sulphur is specifically different from arsenic, but belongs to the same genus. Similarly, all sulphur, and everything that belongs to the same species with sulphur, has the property of coagulating quicksilver; and sometimes succeeds in imparting to it a red colour, and sometimes fails to do so.

We said above that when arsenic is sublimed it gives out globules of quicksilver like grains of millet, which is identical with ordinary quicksilver. For this reason the Sages have endeavoured, by a congruous digestion, to coagulate the same quicksilver with itself, even as gold is coagulated by its intrinsic power. Arsenic, says Geber, has the two metallic first principles, sulphur and quicksilver, combined, and by their means may itself be designated as the first principle of Nature, in virtue of their properties and qualities. In the same book he says that the fetid spirit and living water, which is also called dry water, are the first principles of Nature. There can be no transition from the softness of quicksilver to the hardness of metals, except in some intermediate substance. Hence neither quicksilver by itself, nor sulphur by itself, is the first principle of Nature, but some intermediate matter which contains both. The quicksilver extracted from sulphur and arsenic is, however, more proximately the substance of our Medicine than the same sulphur and arsenic while they remain as they are.

If there be a third nature which contains our quicksilver and sulphur in the most highly purified condition, and without any admixture of other elements, this substance may be regarded as most proximately the first principle of our Medicine.

The arsenic to which Geber refers as the third principle of Nature in the generation of metals is a compound of quicksilver and sulphur, and possesses the virtue and power of both. It cannot be properly called sulphur, nor yet quicksilver, and thus it is true that there are only two principles of Nature. Nor is this arsenic, which has quicksilver for its matter and sulphur for its active potency, in any sense a thing superfluous, but is a sufficing principle of Nature in the generation of metals. Hence the quicksilver of which we speak is not common quicksilver, nor is our sulphur common sulphur; but there is in our quicksilver an occult homogeneous sulphur, and it is by means of this inward sulphur that all our changes are accomplished.

Therefore, do not suppose that any compound but the one I have mentioned is the right substance of our Art, and forbear to spend your labour in vain upon magnesia, marchasite, tutia, antimony, or any other heterogeneous material. Our sulphur is the vital agent which digests and perfects our quicksilver; but the sulphur of marchasite, for instance (as Geber tells us), is only degrading and combustive; in the separation thereof the quicksilver of marchasite is left dead at the bottom of the vessel, and must afterwards be sublimed by fire. Again, we do not find in the composition of gold, or of the other metals, anything that in the least suggests or resembles marchasite. Though arsenic and marchasite are generated from nearly the same elements, their diversity of form has combined and developed those elements in a widely different manner, since the same substance, if differently digested, receives a different form. This is sufficiently patent from the fact that different limbs are generated from the same substance. As with marchasite, so it is with tutia, magnesia, and all other like substances. Thus, through many mistakes, and by a process of elimination, we at length, through the grace of God, arrive at the substance which we firmly believe to be the right one. This short exposition must suffice for the present.

EXTRACTS MADE BY LACINIUS

FROM THE WORKS OF ARNOLD DE VILLA NOVA, IN WHICH THE COMPOSITION OF OUR STONE IS PRACTICALLY AND LUCIDLY SET FORTH.

WE have learned all that Bonus could tell us about the first principles of metals and their generation. We will now proceed to consider, practically and theoretically, the composition of our Stone, since practice and theory are mutually helpful: practice is informed by theory, and theory is corrected and checked by practice. Now, as Arnold de Villa Nova has, in his Rosary, given us a practical treatise on the Philosophers' Stone, I will arrange some of his remarks in chapters according to the following plan:

CHAPTER THE FIRST shews that there is one Philosophers' Stone, because there is one essence, and one method, both in the red and white Medicine. The red Medicine is merely a further development of the white.

CHAPTER THE SECOND shews whence is the Stone extracted. Observe well the answer.

CHAPTER THE THIRD shews the chief difficulty of our work to be the discovery of the first matter of metals.

CHAPTER THE FOURTH shews our first physical object must be to dissolve the Stone into its Mercury, or primal matter of all metals. Hence the philosopher says that we must first be at pains to dissolve and sublime the two luminaries, because the primal grade of operation in our Art is to reduce them to quicksilver. Unless the bodies lose their corporeal nature, and become spiritual, we shall make no progress with our work. The solution of a body takes place through the operation of the spirit, and is attended with the coagulation of the spirit. Then the body mingles with the spirit, and the spirit with the body.

CHAPTER THE FIFTH shews the four principal methods in this Magistery: Dissolution, Purification, Reduction, Fixation. To dissolve is to make the gross subtle; to purify is to make the dark bright; reduction is of the humid into the dry;

fixation is by resolution and coagulation of the spirit into its own body, or solid substance.

CHAPTER THE SIXTH shews the dissolution of the Stone, and its inhumation, which are the first regimen. Dissolution is brought about by purified Mercury. This is done in order that we may have sulphur and Mercury of that matter whereof gold and silver are developed beneath the earth.

CHAPTER THE SEVENTH shews the second regimen: Ablution and purification of the black, corrupt, fetid matter, so that it may become exceeding bright, clear, and spotless—which ablution is performed by division of the Stone into its four elements and the cleansing of each element.

Arnold tells us truly that all metals are generated from quicksilver and sulphur, which coagulate the quicksilver by means of its heat or vapour; since every dry element naturally drinks up its humid element. Quicksilver in its essence is a compound of very subtle, white, sulphureous earth, with bright water, so as to make up one substance, which finds no rest upon a plane surface. It is homogeneous in nature, and is either wholly fixed, or else wholly evaporates in the fire. By constant sublimation it is purified, digested, and thickened, and so gradually coagulated into white and red sulphur. This process of constant dissolution and coagulation is performed by Nature in not less than a thousand years; but Art, through the mediation of Nature, accomplishes it in a very short time. If, then, we would prepare the medicine, we must both accelerate and imitate Nature.

Quicksilver is the matter and element of all metals alike; all of them when melted are converted thereto, and it also combines with them; at the same time, in some it is more and in some less pure, on account of its corruptive external sulphur. But quicksilver is coagulated by virtue of its own inward, non-combustive sulphur. The philosopher tells us that white, incombustible sulphur congeals mercury, and is the best thing that can possibly be used for conversion of mercury into good silver. If the sulphur be pure, good, but, on the other hand, of a red brilliancy, containing the gentle heat without the combustive violence of natural sulphur, it is the best thing that can possibly be used for converting Mercury into the Sun. The result of good quicksilver and impure combustive sulphur is copper. Porous, impure quicksilver and impure sulphur produce iron. Tin has good, pure quicksilver, but its sulphur is bad and ill mixed. Lead has gross, bad, ponderous, and earthy quicksilver, and bad, fetid, and feeble sulphur. So, at least, Aristotle tells us.

The common outward sulphur, then, is the cause of the imperfection of metals. There are two kinds of sulphur in every metal except gold, the outward combustive and the inward non-combustive, which belongs to the substantial composition of the quicksilver. The outward sulphur is separable, and is removed by calcination; the internal sulphur is inseparable from the quicksilver by calcination in fire. The latter the quicksilver retains, nor can it ever be taken away, as being homogeneous with it: the former it spurns and rejects, and exposes to the action of the fire, which consumes it. It is the property of this external sulphur, always either to be burned in the fire, or in its composition with quicksilver to burn, corrupt, and denigrate. It is quicksilver, then, which perfects bodies, and saves them from combustion, because the more bodies are of the nature of quicksilver, the less are they liable to combustion. And as quicksilver prevents combustion, so it is the cause of metallic fusibility, and it is that by means of which the tincture pervades the metals, since it receives the homogeneous tinctural influence in all its smallest parts. Quicksilver adheres most readily to quicksilver, then to gold, then to silver, because these two metals are most homogeneous to it. It is not so with the other metals, till they are purged of their corruptive sulphur.

Those are, then, the most perfect bodies which contain the largest proportion of quicksilver, while those which contain less are less perfect. It contains in itself its own good sulphur, by means of which it is coagulated into gold and silver, but by different methods of digestion. If the sulphur be white, it will digest the quicksilver into silver; if, on the other hand, it shew a red brilliancy, and have a noble but not destructive fire, it will coagulate the quicksilver into gold, and the elixir of gold is composed from it. Observe that both white and red sulphur are in reality the same metallic matter; but they are more and less powerful because of the different degree of their digestion. Hence the philosopher says that all gold has red sulphur, and all silver white sulphur. But this sulphur is not found upon the earth, as Avicenna assures us, otherwise than in these two; hence we most subtly prepare these bodies, that we may have red sulphur and quicksilver of the same matter on the earth of which gold and silver are made under the earth: for these are lucent bodies, whose rays tinge other bodies with true white and red. Thus the red tincture is obtained from gold, and the white tincture from silver.

Chapter I.
Shewing that there is but one Philosophers' Stone.

Arnold de Villa Nova says that there is but one Philosophers' Stone, and there is but one Medicine, to which nothing foreign is added, and from which nothing is removed, except that which is foreign to it. Its external sulphur of vulgar quicksilver is foreign to it; its inward sulphur belongs to its own nature, and into this it must be converted by our magistery. Do not introduce into it, then, any powder, or water, or any other foreign substance, because no heterogeneous material can possibly enter into its composition. If any foreign matter be added to it, it is straightway corrupted, and does not become what you desire. The Stone itself, in order that it may enter the common metals, must attain a state of great fixation and subtleness, that it may become a medicine for corrupt bodies.

Chapter II.
Whence the Physical Stone is extracted.

Our physical Stone, or Medicine, may be obtained from all metals; but it is found in the highest perfection in gold and silver. Without the Sun and its shadow, the Moon, we can have no tinging quicksilver, and he is foolish who attempts to accomplish our Magistery in their absence. On the other hand, he who knows how to tinge quicksilver with the Sun and Moon is in possession of our arcanum, which may become red sulphur, but at first is called white sulphur. Gold is the father, and silver the mother of the proximate substance of our Stone, for out of these bodies, prepared with their sulphur or arsenic, is our medicine elicited. It may, indeed, be possible to derive it from other bodies, but it is found nearer to the hand, and more easily, in quicksilver, which is the father of those lights and the root of all metals. Of this were they all made, and into the same all of them return. That which is now our Stone is not quicksilver, but once formed part of it, and it is this which imparts to it its brightness, preserves it from combustion, and is the cause of its perfection. Do not work with anything except Mercury and the Sun for the Sun, and Mercury and the Moon for the Moon.

Chapter III.

It is impossible for the Stone to be perfected by the substance of metals only.

As water cannot rise above the level of its spring, so the wonderful Tincture, which is to transmute all common metals into gold and silver, cannot possibly be perfected out of the substance of metals only, not even of gold and silver. The elixir must be far more purified and digested than these. If gold and silver gave of their perfection to other metals, they themselves would become imperfect.

The tincture which is to impart perfection to all other metallic bodies must itself possess a superabundance of digestive perfection and matured excellence. Most of our Alchemists leave off with the substance with which they ought to have begun, and consequently nothing comes of their projection.

Chapter IV.

On the first Operation of our Magistery.

Our first business, according to Arnold, must be to dissolve our Stone into its Mercury or first matter. Species can be transmuted only by the reduction of their matter to the generic First Matter. Hence we must reduce our Stone to quicksilver. By the projection of our Tincture, the species, or properties of the species, are not changed, but only individual quantities of metal belonging to the species. Silver as a metallic species is never changed into gold, which has immediately its own species, but individuals of this or another metallic species may well so change. Your first step, then, must be to bring about the dissolution of gold and silver into quicksilver. Hence the Sages say: Unless the bodies become incorporeal, and the spirits corporeal, no progress will be made. The true beginning, then, of our work is the solution of our body, because bodies, when dissolved, become spiritual in their nature, and are yet at the same time more fixed than the spirit, though they are dissolved with it. For the solution of the body means the coagulation of the spirit, and vice versa; each gives up something of its own nature: they meet each other half-way, and thus become one inseparable substance, like water mixed with water.

Chapter V.
On the Perfect Investigation of the Physical Stone.

It is clear, then, that the operation of our Stone is the operation of Nature.

As ice is water because it is dissolved into water, so our Stone, which is dissolved into quicksilver, is thereby proved to be quicksilver. Our operation is a conversion of the elements, an amicable conjunction of the humid with the dry, and of the cold with the hot. But the dry becomes humid, and the cold becomes hot, only by means of an intermediate substance. If, then, the dry be converted into the cold, and the cold into the humid, and the humid into the hot, and the hot into the dry, then you have the whole Magistery. The four stages of our work, then, are solution, purification, reduction, and fixation, the significance of which terms has already been explained. Solution is of the gross into the subtle; purification is of the dark into the bright; reduction is of the humid into the dry; fixation is of the volatile over its own body. Let the Stone, therefore, be dissolved with best Mercury, purged from its terrestrial and humid nature, by means of sublimation, and afterwards reduced. With this let it be twice pounded, and then placed in the *Balneum Mariæ*.

How Mercury is Cleansed.

Sublime your Mercury once or twice with vitriol and salt, till its substance is very white and brilliant. When it is in a volatile state, plunge it into boiling water, till it once more becomes quicksilver; remove the water, and proceed to use it for our Magistery. Pound it, soak it in its own water, and digest it in S. Mary's bath; distil it through a filter. Watch for a black oil appearing on the surface, which is the true sign of the dissolution being completed. Watch it well, I repeat, lest it evaporate into smoke, and what you do with the white, do also with the red. The difference between the Solar and the Lunar Medicine is this, that the Solar includes the Lunar, but the Lunar does not include the Solar, the Solar having in addition a reddish or golden colouring substance. Be patient and do not attempt to extract the Tincture in a hurry; haste burns up, instead of maturing and digesting, our substance. Bear in mind that the chief error in this Art is haste, which ends in the combustion of everything. Much fire at the beginning is to the detriment of the tincture, and consumes the medicine.

Pound and cook with patience, and reiterate the process again and again, because that which is soaked with water is softened. The more you pound the substance, the softer it will become, and the softer it becomes, the more the gross parts are subtilized, till perfect union of body and spirit supervenes. For by means of pounding and softening and digestion, the parts held together by the viscosity of the water in bodies are separated. Bodies that are dissolved, are reduced to the nature of spirits, and their union is thenceforward indissoluble, like that of water mixed with water: for Nature rejoices when the bridegroom is united to the bride. Things which cannot be dissolved are devoid of subtle or soft parts. I pray you, therefore, labour in the dissolution of the Stone, disintegrating the grosser parts that the gross may be rejected and the work performed with the subtle.

Chapter VI.

On the Inhumation of the Stone.

When the Stone is dissolved, expose the whole of it to gentle heat, for its better putrefaction and digestion, and for the consummation of the connubial rite, during the space of a month of the Sages, *i.e.*, of thirty days, since the danger of combustion is removed by digestion and inhumation. Let all be boiled together over a gentle fire, till the whole substance resolves into its first matter, and becomes truly like quicksilver. The sign that the solution is complete, is a blackness, which appears after a certain time, which also we denominate the Raven's Head.

When the Stone is fully dissolved in S. Mary's Bath, it should be passed through a filter. The blackness is a sign that the process of volatilization is accomplished.

Recapitulation of the First Regimen.

Sublime the Mercury, and dissolve it; then subject the whole substance to coction, till it is reduced to its first nature, *i.e.*, till we have sulphur and quicksilver, of the same matter which in mines is digested into gold and silver. And he that has this Magistery has an everlasting treasure.

Chapter VII.
The second Regimen, or that of Purification.

The second regimen of the Stone is its ablution, that is to say, the removal of all that is black, corrupt, and fetid in it, whereby it is rendered very brilliant, and clear, and pure. This is brought about by the division of the elements, the distillation of the waters, and the solution of the Stone, because there are two dry or stony, and two humid or watery elements. The dry elements are fire and earth, the aqueous are air and water. Fire purifies water by distillation, and thus all the elements cleanse and become assimilated to each other. So is our Stone divided into four elements, that it may be the better subtilised, and cleansed from stains, and afterwards more firmly conjoined. But nothing ever was born, has grown, or is animated, except after putrefaction and digestion. If there be no putrefaction, there can be no melting and no solution, but if there be no solution, then nothing is accomplished.

Division of the Stone into four Elements.

Take the Stone in its putrefied state, cleanse it by the cleansing of the four elements, by distillation, by a light and equable fire. Take the water. Then increase the fire a little, till all the air is mixed with fire, and that which remains at the bottom, in a burnt state, is dry, black earth. The water is cleansed in the bath of S. Mary, but air and fire are distilled through the ashes, and the grosser parts of the earth remain below, while the more subtle parts are carried upward. Earth desiccates and fixes, water purifies and cleanses. Air and fire tinge, and cause fluidity; hence it is necessary to have much water and air. The quantity of the Tincture will be in proportion to the quantity of air. Seek, therefore, my dearest, in all thy works to overcome Mercury in commixtion, that thou mayest have enough of air; and if thou art able to perfect this by itself, thou will be the explorer of the conquering potency which resides in the highest perfection of Nature. After this operation it is still necessary for the Medicine to be matured and nourished over the fire, as the child is nourished at the breast.

On the Ablution of Water.

When you have separated the elements of the Stone, cleanse them; cleanse the air and water by a sevenfold distillation. The fire and earth, on the other hand, must be well calcined. Distil the air and water separately, for the air is more precious than the water. The air tinges the earth, and infuses into it life and the sensible soul. Air and water must be guarded from excessive heat, or they will be dried up. This is brought about by inhumation. When the purification is complete, the whole substance is wonderfully white and brilliant. The sediment of the water in distillation must be carefully removed and set apart with the blackness of the earth, already mentioned. Set also apart the seven times distilled water, for the same is the Medicine and the Water of Life which washes the Laton. As you do with the white water. so do also with the red; there is no difference between the two, except that one tinges white, and the other red.

On the Ablution of Air.

Separate the air from the fire by distillation, viz., through the ashes. That which is distilled is most pure air; that which remains at the bottom, is dry fire. The air is the oil and tincture, the gold and soul of the Sages, the ointment by means of which the whole Magistery is effected. Fire and air must be distilled together because they are of the same nature. If you mix the Stone with fire, it will be red, and have all the virtues of the Red Tincture.

How oil is extracted from all things.

Place over the body, whence you wish to extract oil, sufficient purified Mercury to cover it completely, that is, to the height of four inches, or better if more; then put it over a slow fire. The oil, or air, will soon begin to bubble up through the quicksilver. Collect it carefully, and, if necessary, that is, should the quicksilver begin to diminish, add more pure and warm quicksilver and continue the coction till all the oil has been obtained. This oil must then be purified by inhumation and sevenfold distillation through the alembic, till it be brilliantly white. It will float on the surface of our water. Set it apart, for it is the Oily Tincture, the Golden Soul, and the Unguent of the Philosophers, which colours, tinges, fixes, and makes fluid. A thin plate of metal steeped into it, will be changed into silver if it be of the white, and into gold if it be of the red grade.

But do not mix the oil of gold with the oil of silver, or the reverse; for each has its own special purpose, one to tinge white, and the other to tinge red.

Difference between Water and Oil.

Water only cleanses, oil tinges and colours. If you dip a rag in clean water, it will become cleaner than it was; but the water will evaporate. If you dip it in coloured oil, it will be saturated with the colour of the oil, and you will be able to remove this colour only by burning the whole rag. For oil is thicker and more intense, and yet, at the same time, lighter than water. Nevertheless, it is by means of water, and from water, that we obtain this oil. The water is the spirit, which retains the oil, or soul, as the soul retains the body. Through the oil our coagulation is effected, because it retains the volatile substance. Sow the soul in white flaky earth, for it will retain it: since, when it has ascended from earth to heaven, and descended to the earth, it will have received the strength of things above, and of things below.

The cleansing of Fire and Earth.

Collect the impure sediments obtained from the cleansing of the oil, and place them with the fire, since they are fire, and have blackness and redness which must be pounded with the first water, and gently burned till they become a dry powder, without any of the humidity of air. So, also, the sediment of water must be combined with earth, and thrice calcined till it becomes white and dry. Calcine fire with fire, and earth with earth, till they are pure and free from blackness; what ascends from the fire is the red oil; what ascends from the earth is the white precious oil. Perform all these processes, and preserve each part carefully by itself.

The cause of ablution according to Plato.

According to Plato, you should to the fullest extent of your ability effect the separation of the elements: cleanse water and air by distillation, and earth by heat and calcination, till nothing of the soul is left in the body, *i.e.*, when nothing more evaporates from it, if placed on a red-hot metallic plate. In no part of our operation do we need any water but our white water, nor any oil but our white or orange-coloured oil, nor any fire except our red fire, nor any earth except that which is pallid or slightly white. But if you thus prepare the elements, the earth will be ready for solution, the water efficacious for digestion, and the oil, in which is the fire, eminently fitted for tinging. If the end of your process should not present you with such elements, this is an indication of error; set about the correction thereof, for it will be easier than beginning again. Keep each element carefully sealed up in a well-stoppered jar, write upon each its own name, and a record of its properties, for it would be fatal to mistake one for the other.

On the third Regimen, which is that of Reduction.

The third regimen consists in bringing back the humid water to the dry earth, that it may recover its lost humidity. Since fire and earth are both dry elements, they must first be combined before this restoration can take place. Then the dry elements will be in a condition to drink up more moisture than they had before, for calcination disintegrates a body and so empties it of all moisture, that it will imbibe its aqueous humidity very greedily.

Arnold here places a chapter on the albification and sublimation of the earth by frequent pounding, imbibition, and digestion of the Mercury. When this process is fully accomplished, that is, when it ascends white as snow, we have the good, flaky, brilliantly white earth, or the white incombustible sulphur. If you wish to obtain red sulphur, dissolve this white sulphur in red water, by means of pounding, and saturation, and good decoction; coagulate it alternately into a stone and alternately dissolve what is coagulated in the red water. After the third time, sublime the whole in a fierce fire, and that which rises upward will be snowy white sulphur, while that which remains at the bottom will be red, like scarlet. Hence you see that while there are two different stages of our magistery, there is in reality only one Stone.

The true method of bringing back the Water to the Earth.

Pour at first upon the earth (which you have carefully pounded) one-fiftieth part its own quantity of water; for it is necessary at the beginning to give the earth little water, just as an infant has to be given at first little nutriment, and then gradually more. This should be repeated over and over again, with great patience, more and more water being poured over the earth each time, but not more than the earth can conveniently drink up; after each trituration and effusion, the whole should be subjected to thorough coction for eight days at a time. Without constant, patient irrigation the earth cannot bring forth fruit. Continue the trituration and assation until all the water has been absorbed and dried up, while the earth has become white. The water is to be administered temperately after each calcination; too much of it will produce a tempestuous condition; too little will convert the matter into glowing ashes. The degree of heat applied should be that of horse dung. After imbibition, it should be inhumed for seven days. There are three colours, marking the three stages of this process. The black colour shews that the substance is still imperfect: after its appearance the heat of the fire should be slightly increased. By constantly repeating the process you will soon make the earth white; and then you should behold the orange colour. The more limpid the water, the more limpid the earth will be; the more the earth is washed, the whiter it will become.

Things are sublimed either by themselves, if they are spirits, or, if bodies, they are sublimed by means of some spiritual substance. Our earth is not sublimed in its condition as calx, unless it be first subtly incorporated with mercury. Hence you should pound the earth, saturate it with mercury, and digest them till they become one body. This must be repeated over and over again, or else the sublimation cannot take place, because the earth will not be properly incorporated with the mercury. Sublimation is contingent upon the reduction of the body into a subtle matter and nature. By means of this sublimation bodies are freed from their grosser elements, and reduced to their first matter, which can then be perfectly developed. If you wish to develop the sublimed substance into silver, both earth and mercury should be white: if you wish to develop it into gold, they should both be red, and the powder should be incerated. When Mercury is sublimed for the Moon, nothing else should be mixed with it, for the colour of the Sun does not enter into the Moon, nor that of the Moon into the Sun. Do not mix that which ascends and that which remains below. That which remains below should be again pounded and saturated, till the whole is sublimed or incorporated with Mercury. In the sublimation of Mercury you will see a most white earth, like snow, and, as it were, a dead powder adhering to the sides of the aludel. Reiterate sublimation thereon, without the fæces remaining below, Soon that which ascends will settle in the shape of a white, flaky powder. These are the superior ashes, while that which remains below is the foul sediment, and should be removed. In this way the white sulphur or white tincture is perfected.

The fourth Regimen, which consists in Fixation, and for this purpose we need a certain Ferment.

The fourth operation is to fix the white and red sulphur over a fixed body, *i.e.*, silver and gold respectively. Without a proper ferment the Moon cannot become the Sun, but the substance, having nothing to prevent it from doing so, will again revert into water. It must therefore be incorporated with the body from which it was first prepared, viz., the Moon or the Sun. It is necessary, in fact, to unite it to its own proper body. For this purpose mix it with the ferment (either white or red), which will completely assimilate it to its own nature. Do not mix the ferment of one (white) sulphur with another (red) sulphur: the result would be disappointing. The ferment of gold is gold, and the ferment of silver is silver, and there are no other proper ferments in all the world, because nothing fixes which is not itself fixed.

The weight of the Ferment must exceed, or at least be equal to, the weight of its Sulphur.

The quantity of volatile sulphur in any ferment must not be greater than that of its body. If there be a preponderance of the body, says Plato, it will quickly change the volatile sulphur into a powder of its own colour, *i.e.*, either that of gold or of silver. The sulphur cannot enter the bodies except through the medium of water, the intermediate substance between the sulphur and the ferment. Therefore put first the earth, then the water, and then the air (Avicenna). If you wish to obtain the red

Tincture, put in the fourth place fire, since the white Tincture needs only three elements, but the red Tincture needs fire as well. Open, therefore, and seal, solve and coagulate, wash and dry, for water is the medium which joins the tinctures of oil, air, and fire. If you first take oil and then earth, the oil will mortify in the earth, for the water will enter. If you first take water and then oil, the oil will float upon the water. But if you first take water and afterwards earth, the water will outweigh the earth. Fix, therefore, the water with the earth till it adheres to it. If one of the four be destroyed, all will die; if one have more soul than another, it will be worthless. The ferment is the soul, see that you arrange fermentation so as to produce a calcined, dissolved, and indurated dust. If the fermentation be not rightly performed, the whole Magistery will fail.

The practical uses of dividing the elements.

If you do not divide the Stone into its four elements, the soul cannot well be united to the body. If you do not mix of the body with that over which you desire to make the projection, the body will not love the spirit. If you do not combine the ferment with the elixir, the body over which the projection is made is not properly coloured. If you do not sublime all you put into the elixir, it will be rough gold and silver, and if the whole be not prepared, it will not sustain the fire. Finally, without pains in softening and hardening, the gold and silver will want ductility in operating. The earth which is put into the elixir must be sublimed, in order that the whole may be completely united. If you wish to project the elixir, make earth of that substance whose body you wish to change, and put in the ferment (as above), if it be gold, of gold, and if it be silver, of silver. You must combine the ferment with the body on which you desire to project the elixir. The body and the ferment which are combined in the elixir must be a powder twice or thrice sublimed. Each sublimation will intensify the virtue of the elixir, namely, one upon a hundred, a hundred upon a thousand, and so on to infinity.

We must be careful about the proper quantity of each substance.

If you wish to prepare our Stone, you should know how much water, and air, and fire, and earth it contains when it is calcined, when it is dissolved, and when it is reduced respectively. In the first case, there will be greater dryness, greater heat, less moisture, less cold. In the second, there will be greater cold, less heat, more moisture, and less dryness. In the third, there will be greater heat, less moisture, more dryness, and less cold.

How the Elements are improved, and how the Fusion of the Medicine is affected.

In the conjunction of the Stone, expect three principal colours, first the black, then the white, then the red. Take care that the tincture does not become red before it becomes black, for then it will perish by combustion, and that none of the colours appear before their proper time, or out of their proper order. Should the red appear before the black, or before the white, decoct the whole in white water till the proper colour is restored. Note also that decoction by inhumation obviates the error of combustion, and restores lost humidity. If the medicine does not combine properly, correct by dissolution. The purification and dissolution are brought about, not by common, but by mercurial water. We calcine the medicine that we may the better dissolve it, that it may the better be cleansed, fixed, and melted, and that the bodies may receive a better impression therefrom, and may be more fully permeated thereby. Towards the end of the Magistery, it is a good plan to dissolve the body of the ferment, whether white or red, in order that it may amalgamate all the more readily. Not all the parts are separated in dissolution, but the separation is sufficiently complete to ensure the removal of all impurities. If the metal which is to be changed by means of the Medicine, have not sufficient colour, more of the Medicine should be added; if it have too much, the dose should be smaller. If the Medicine be not sufficiently fixed, the remedy lies in repeating the dissolution and coagulation several times. If it be too firm, more of oil, that is, the air of the Stone, should be added; and observe, as a general rule, that for fixation you must have more of the cold and dry, and less of the hot and humid elements.

Of the quantities to be observed in Fixation.

All Nature is ruled by ratio and proportion; hence, in the fixation of our Stone, we must know how much we need of water, air, earth, and fire. If the right proportions are not observed, your whole work will be a failure. Either too much or too little of earth, air, fire, and water would entail some corresponding defect. I speak here of elixirs in general, but fire is not introduced as an element of the white elixir. The heavy elements in our substance and the ferment are called earth : those which rise upward are described as air and water. For fixation into earth, in the case of the white Tincture, there should always be more of earth than of the other elements. If there be 1½ oz. of air, and 2 ozs. of water, there must be 2¾ ozs. of earth, and thrice as much of the ferment of earth as there is of white sulphur. If there be 1 oz. of white sulphur, there must be 3 ozs. of the ferment. Add 2 ozs. of water, 1½ oz. of air, and the elixir will be complete. For the solar Tincture, which is of hotter quality than that of the Moon, we need 2 ozs. of earth, 3 of water, as many of air, and 1½ oz. of fire—for if there be much water and little fire, the fire will be extinguished. The heavy elements, like earth and water, are more useful for the purpose of producing fixation and rest; the lighter elements, viz., air and fire, are more useful for the purposes of fusion and of the Tincture. Do not eat what you do not drink, neither drink what you do not eat, but eat and drink one after the other according to the requirements of our art.

On the Fixation and Composition of the White Elixir.

No body which has not first been purified can possibly retain its soul. Let there be drinking after eating, not *vice versa*. Fix well, mix well, tinge well, and you have the whole Magistery. Pound three parts of pure powdered silver well with twice its quantity of white quicksilver in a mortar of porphyry, till the Mercury has drunk up all the silver, and the compound is of the consistency of butter. Purify it with vinegar and common salt, till the vinegar comes out pure and clear; then wash away the salt with clean, sweet water, and dry before the fire. Pound it with one part of the white sulphur till the two become one body, incerate it with one part of its white water, and sublime little by little over the fire, till all that is volatile in it has ascended upward; take it out when cool and collect the particles which have settled on the sides of the vessel; then repeat the process of pounding, saturation, and sublimation—constantly reducing that which ascends upward to that which lies fixed below; till all is fixed, which is naturally brought about by the coagulative virtue of the fixed sulphur. In short, study Nature, and supply her with all necessary outward conditions: then you may trust to her to do the rest. When your earth is impregnated you may expect a birth in Nature's own good time; when the birth has taken place, nourish and strengthen it to support the fire, and you will be able to make projections.

Of the Reduction of Air upon the White Elixir.

When the water is fixed with the earth, pound it, saturate it by sprinkling with one part of its air, sublime it with a gradually increasing fire, till by constant sublimation the whole is fixed. Then expose it to a good fire for twenty-four hours, to a still fiercer fire for another day and night, and to a very fierce fire, proper for melting, on the third day and night. The air will then be fixed with the earth and water.

Inceration of the White Elixir.

Take one drachm of the crystal plate which you find at the bottom of the vessel; pound it, and drop on it slowly, in a thin crucible, over a gentle fire, some of its white air, till it becomes liquid, like wax, without any smoke. Test upon a hot plate, and if it melt swiftly like wax, the ceration is complete. If not, complete the process by dropping its white oil gradually thereon, till it becomes like smokeless melted wax. Continue the sublimation until the whole substance is fixed. That is, when by sublimation you have fixed the purest part of the earth, reiterate the sublimation upon the unfixed part over the fixed part, until all is fixed. Try its fusibility over a good fire; if the result be satisfactory, the sublimation need not be continued. If not, continue sublimation in respect of the unfixed part. Then let it cool, and you have a priceless Tincture, one part of which—with salt dissolved in vinegar—

will transmute 1,000 parts of Mercury, or common metal, into the purest silver, better than that of the mine.

The Composition of the Red Elixir.

The Red Elixir—for changing metals into gold—is prepared in the same way as the White Elixir, gold being in this case substituted for silver. For every white thing substitute a red thing of the same kind; in the place of powdered silver put powdered gold, and the water of Mercury made red with the fire of the Stone. Sublime the substance again and again till all the quicksilver has become fixed. When three-quarters of the red water are fixed, place the whole for twenty-four hours over a very gentle fire, that it may be the better cleansed and fixed. Remove it subsequently, and cerate in a crucible, also over a very slow fire. Drop upon it its red oil, till it becomes liquid as wax without smoke. One part of this Red Tincture projected upon silver, or purified quicksilver—with salt and vinegar—changes 1,000 parts of either into the purest gold, better than that of the mine, and withstanding every test. Hence the Sages say that their gold and silver are not as the gold and silver of the multitude, seeing that they are distinguished by infinitely greater purity.

On the Multiplication of the Medicines.

If you dissolve those medicines, after their fixation and saturation, with their white or red oils, till they flow like wax, and then in their white or red Mercury, till they look like clear water, and afterwards coagulate them by gentle digestion, and again make them liquid with their oils over the fire till they flow very swiftly, their virtue in projection will be doubled. If, when they are dissolved, you distil them once, their powers are multiplied an hundred fold. To multiply the medicines, dissolve the spirit of each respectively in its water by inhumation, separate from each its oil by distillation, then their water, then their fire, and the earth will remain below. Reduce the water by sublimation over the earth, till it is fixed with the earth; then saturate it with the oil, or air, and the tincture till it is fixed and liquid like wax; its virtue will then be multiplied tenfold; repeat the operation, and its virtue will each time be enhanced 100, 1,000, 10,000 fold, etc. The oftener the Medicine is dissolved, sublimed, and coagulated, the more potent it becomes; in each sublimation its projective virtue is multiplied by ten.

What do we mean by Dissolution and Sublimation?

When I speak of solution, you must not think that the elixir is to be altogether resolved into water, but is only to be subtilized as far as possible to have its parts divided, that which is dry in it made humid, and that which is gross made simple, since dissolution is practised for the work of subtilization only, but not sublimation, and for the purpose of uniting the body and the spirit. The subtilization of bodies is the dissolution into water, because distillation or dissolution educes the Stone from potentiality into effect, in which the body and the spirit meet each other halfway, and are thus inseparably conjoined. The confirmation of spirits with bodies takes place when bodies are subtilized, for not otherwise will these retain the spirits. I have not said too much; but if there be anything in my remarks which you do not understand, read then over again and again, until you have become completely possessed of my meaning. What we have said is the strict rule of truth, and you must not depart from it either to the right or to the left, or you will go wrong. If you do not understand my meaning, do not blame me, but your own ignorance.

How to make the Projection.

Now, seeing that it is a matter of some difficulty to melt a million parts together, when you wish to make projection proceed as follows: Take a hundred parts of Mercury, cleansed with vinegar and salt; place it in a crucible over the fire; when it begins to bubble up, add one part of your Elixir, and project the whole upon one hundred other parts of boiling purified Mercury. Then project one part of this entire mixture upon one hundred parts of purified Mercury, and the whole will be turned into our Elixir. Then project one part of this last, coagulated, upon hundred parts of purified Mercury, and it will become the purest gold, or silver, according as the Tincture is red or white. And this is the Rosary of the Philosophers, bearing fragrant roses, both white and red, the essential extract of many books, having nothing superfluous, omitting nothing needful, for the infinite production of true Sun and Moon. Our Medicine has also power to heal all infirmity and diseases, both of inflammation and debility; it turns an old man into a youth. If the illness be of one month's standing, it may be cured in a day; if of one year's standing, it may be healed in twelve days; if of many years' standing, it may be healed in a month. Hence this Medicine is not without reason prized above all other treasures that this world affords.

Recapitulation of the whole work.

First sublime the substance, and purge it of all corrupting impurity; dissolve also, therewith, its white or red additament till the whole is as subtle and volatile as it can possibly become. Then fix it by all methods till it is able to stand the test of the fire. After that, sublime the fixed part of the Stone together with its volatile part; make the fixed volatile, and the volatile fixed, by alternate solution and sublimation; so continue, and then fix them both together till they form a white or red liquid Tincture. In this way you obtain the priceless arcanum which is above all the treasures of the world. Give yourself wholly to this study; meditate on it day and night; and, above all, check the truth of your theoretic notions by constant reference to practice. You will not find in all the books of the Sages anything clearer and plainer than what I have told you. Praise to the Trinity and glory to the Blessed Virgin Mary.

END OF THE COLLECTANEA OF ARNOLD.

Epitome of the Work of Raymondus Lullius, by Lacinius the Calabrian.

IF I could do what my kindly feelings towards the students of this work prompt me to do, I would copy out all the works of Raymondus Lullius. As it is, I must be content with giving you an abridgment of his letter to King Rupert, which is as lucid and clear as it is short. This treatise is an epitomised summary of all his works, as he himself calls it, and is therefore both brief and weighty.

Letter or Epitome of Raymondus Lullius.

Since this art is beset with a possibility of error and misunderstanding on every side, I have striven as far as possible to express myself so clearly and accurately as to preclude all risk of misapprehension. I do not doubt that you, King Rupert, have read all my books, and pondered them well, but you ask me to provide you with an epitome of everything that I have said, in order that you may the more readily carry it in your mind, and I gladly comply with your request. I received your letter at Vienna. But not till after my arrival at Salerno do I find myself able to attend to it. If you are not satisfied with my method, you must needs seek one that is shorter.

[Raymondus is here speaking of the method of his master, Arnold. For Raymondus divided the elements, and subtilized spirit and body in a different way from that which Arnold delivered to him, though, of course, the substance of the Stone, and the substantial mode of procedure, were the same with both.]

You ask which of the three Stones is more useful, readily obtained, and efficacious: Well, the mineral method is long and full of risks. It consists in two waters, one of which makes the Stone volatile without labour or danger; the other fixes it, and is fixed with it, and this operation is attended with risk. This latter water is extracted from a certain fetid menstruum; it is stronger than any other water, and the danger consists in the ease with which, in ablution, its spirit may escape.

The Animal Stone is far more difficult of composition, so that far greater knowledge is required for it; yet it enables you not only to transmute metals into gold, but to change anything into any other thing, whence the potency of this Stone is infinite. The Vegetable Stone takes still longer to prepare, and has still more wonderful virtues than the Animal Stone. It should follow the Animal Stone as far as the rectification of elements, and, if thus prepared, its effect passes into the animal. Everything transmuted by means of the Vegetable Stone, far transcends Nature in excellence and size, because it is impregnated with the quintessence which performs so many wonderful things in the world.

All alchemical gold is composed from corrosives, and from the incorruptible quintessence which is fixed with the ferment by the skill of the artist. Such quintessence is a certain mortified and empoisoned spirit in the Mineral Stone. The Animal Stone may be the most miraculous medicine for the human body, just as if it were an extract of human blood. The quintessence which is in the Vegetable Stone restores youth, and preserves the human body from all accidental corruption. The spirit of the quintessence, as you know, is that which tinges and transmutes, if it be mixed with its proper ferment. The Vegetable Stone is more noble, and useful, and efficacious, than all the rest.

You ask me whether the work can be shortened; I tell you that all abbreviation diminishes perfection, so that the medicine which is composed by accurtation has less transmutatory power. There is, however, a multiplex accurtation of the Mineral Stone. In order to curtail its effect as little as possible, you should after the first calcination and putrefaction, which is performed with the most limpid and clear first water during a space of twenty days, and not less, separate from the substance a red powder, and distil it with the second water so as to prevent the escape of the spirit. Take only the last part of this water, after rubefaction in the alembic. Dissolve therein the powders, by placing both in hot water in a sealed vessel; then set over it an alembic, and distil as much as will ascend. This water pour away; that which remains with the body coagulate in a well-closed vessel among hot ashes; make other water and pour over it; then distil and coagulate ten times. Thus the Stone will be made perfect. If you wish to increase its efficiency, you may go on distilling and coagulating it as often as you like, or until it is impossible to congeal the body further. This Medicine will change metals into gold, and may be completed in 80 days at the most.

In the case of the Animal Stone,

there is no possibility of abridgment, except, indeed, that the earth may be ruled with fire, and the water with air, when its efficacy will be the same; this is called the accurtation of middle time. As to the Vegetable Stone, the same may be said. The following directions will be found useful in the preparation of this Stone.

Take the black which is blacker than black, and distil of it 18 parts in a silver vessel, and in the way suggested in my Testament. At the first distillation take only 1½ part, distil it again, and then its 4th part, which also distil a third time; of this again take 2 parts for the fourth distillation, in which take a little less than the whole; distil this 8 or 9 times. Then take a pair of equal sized vessels with narrow mouths, to each of which an alembic is attached. Let a cucurbite also be fitted to one of the alembics. Put in each mouth one pound of this water and one oz. of ferment; place the vessels on a gentle fire, or a furnace the heat of which can be properly regulated. The ferment will be dissolved. Wet sponges with cold water, and tie them over the tubes of the alembic. The ferment, when quite dissolved, will ascend with its water, and the contents of the two vessels communicating will be distilled from one into the other, twice every day, and twice every night, one pound remaining all the time in each vessel. For as much as ascends from one vessel enters it from the other. By this continual heat the body is subtilized, and the spirit condensed. The gentler the fire, and the slower the distillation, the more perfectly is the process performed. Continue this operation for 20 or 22 days, and the quintesssence of this Blessed Water will then be so thickened as not to ascend any more, for then it is fixed with the ferment and changed into the Stone. Take out of the distilling-vessels and place in horse-dung, or the bath. Then dissolve and coagulate in the same night, and repeat this thrice or oftener. The Stone will then be most precious in divine virtue and exalted power.

If you take the White Ferment, the quintessence will be coagulated in 10 days; but it is not so easily dissolved as the Solar Ferment. This process is one of the most subtle in Nature or Art, though the Elixir has not the properties assigned to it by the Sages, viz., that if you mix this complete medicine with any metal, and the product with another metal, the whole will be turned, according to the first principle, into the Lunar Medicine. and if the Sun be added thereto, this also will be converted into the Moon. Such property is not found in our Medicine if prepared in the way described. The quintessence is fixed permanently in the ferment to which it is joined, and transmutes in accordance with the ferment. If, after the tenth distillation, you dissolve gold in our water; then volatilize the water over a slow fire, and place the gold in a humid spot, it will be dissolved of its own accord in four days; and this solution is

Potable Gold, which has such wonderful virtue in the conservation of human life.

If you add to this dissolved gold a paste of quicksilver seven times sublimed with vitriol (the proportion of the gold being one part to seven of the quicksilver), and continue to sublime the mixture over the fœces till fixation takes place, you will have a penetrant and tingent Medicine. If you put one oz. of this liquid gold by itself for eight days over a very gentle fire, with 100 parts of Mercury, it will coagulate the whole into gold. All these wonders are brought about by the spirit of the water which is indissolubly fixed with the gold, in the solution of the gold.

Distil the Vegetable Stone till there is no viscosity in the water. This is the case after the fifth distillation. You will then have the best transparent vitriol and the best cinaprium in equal parts, which combine, triturate, dry in the sun, and after upon coals, till all the aquosity has departed. Project your water thereon. Distil it over a slow and gradually increasing fire: thus the spirit of the quintessence of vitriol, and cinaprium, or antimony, which mainly constitutes the Mineral Stone, is mixed with the spirit of our blessed ardent water, which spirit is the soul of the Vegetable Stone. Repeat the distillation ten times, always letting the bodies be dry before you add the water. Let the spirit remain, and by means of the fire be joined to the spirit of the burning water. When you have accomplished the 10th distillation, counting from the first distillation of the ardent water, add gold in the proportions explained above for the work of the Vegetable Stone. Place in the furnace. In ten days the fixation will be completed, whereas, in the ordinary vegetable process, twenty-five are required. This abridgment does not impair the virtue of the Stone for transmuting metals, but reduces its medicinal potency. Yet, of course, the Medicine will be better and more efficacious all round, if it be prepared in the ordinary, more tedious manner.

When you have thus produced fixation, perform the dissolution in the bath, just as in the case of the Vegetable Stone. But this composite stone is not dissolved so quickly as the Vegetable itself; yet is it quicker dissolved than is the Mineral, namely, in nine days. A penetrating and well-fixed medicine is the best for all purposes; the more quickly it penetrates bodies, the more readily is it joined to them, and the more thorough is its action. Out of fine black lead of the Sages you may extract a certain oil of a golden colour, which if used for the dissolution of the Stone, whether mineral, composite, or animal, after its fixation, and solution for 3 or 4 days, will enable you to dispense with all other solution and coagulation. For this is the occult oil which makes our Medicine petretrable, friendly, and capable of union with all bodies. If you know how to free this oil of its water; and treat it in the manner suggested, you can evolve from it the Stone in thirty days. But in regard to the Vegetable Stone this oil is not needed, because there the processes are expeditious enough. From this brief epistle I must leave you to gather what you want. Farewell.

Notes of Lacinius on the Epistle of Raymondus.

Let me state, in explanation of Raymond's Epistle, that all his works are full of that Vegetable Stone, which he often calls Vegetable Mercury, the water of life, the menstruum, and the menstrual blood, and of which he says that it has the properties of a body, and is produced, as it were, out of the female seed: it is both generative and nutritive, and it causes the growth of gold and silver, educing them from potentiality into activity, and thus at length changing them into the Stone. If it causes gold, etc., to grow, it must be by its dissolution—hence it is that which dissolves bodies, which, however, must first be calcined and volatilized. But this cannot be done by a vegetable product, as foolish persons suppose, but with things of a like nature. Raymondus distinctly discountenances such a view. He says that the whole mystery of the mineral way consists in two waters, one of which volatilizes the Stone (which is fixed), while the other water fixes it again, and is also fixed with it by the skill of the artist. The quintessence which composes the whole Stone is fixed and fortified according to the ferment joined to it, and performs transmutation accordingly. But it is possible to fix the quintessence over its own earth and join it with the metal; yet this method does not find favour with Raymondus, because when it is fixed upon another ferment, the work is performed quicker, its potency is greater, and it is more natural.—What Raymondus here alludes to as the quintessence, is by Rhasis described under the name of armoniac salt. With his menstruum, or salt, Raymond extracts from metals their souls, which he calls sulphur of Nature. He causes them to ascend and cling to the sides of the vessels by means of fire. The extract he often terms the metallic sperm, from which again he extracts the four elements, with his circulatory celestial medicines, by the help of digestions and distillations. These elements he fixes, solves, and coagulates on his earth; and thus he composes the Stone.

For the present you may operate in the following manner. Make a water out of dry vitriol, saltpetre, and cinabrium. Sublime one pound of this water with half-a-pound of cinabrium three times, always adding fresh cinabrium. Then rectify it by itself that it may be well purified. Take that pure water, and mix with it as much acuated vegetable water with its sublimed earth; mix them gradually and carefully, and let them stand in a well-sealed vessel for twenty-four hours. Then distil all the water in a bath; pour it on again, and distil again, till the mineral spirit is well united to the vegetable spirit, and you will see them lying at the bottom like a piece of ice. Pour away the distilled water since we need it no more. The strength of the ice, or spirit, you can intensify by repeated distillations in the bath, with more water. Put one pound of aqua fortis over one ounce of that salt—do the same with the water of life, which must be highly rectified, and you can increase the potency of the ice, or rather fire, almost indefinitely.

Take of this ice one pound, pound it with one ounce of volatile Sol, reduced to the nature of a spirit, by the mediation of menstrual water conformed to its nature. Now this water, which volatilizes the Stone, is not really water of life. But when you have gold or silver thus volatile or foliate, the same is disposed for dissolving or uniting with the ice. Distil for eight days in the bath, and the whole is dissolved into a liquid of a golden colour; make it circulate for twenty days in the double vessel; it will then coagulate as a ruby-coloured Stone; distil, dissolve, and coagulate, and you have the Medicine.

Extracts made by Lacinius from the Lights of Lights by Rhasis.

SOLUTION is the root of Alchemy. Hence we must discover the natural solvents and coagulants. We will, therefore, proceed to speak of soluble and solvent mineral substances-- of atraments and alums, of mineral spirits, of metals and precious stones—their nature, the method of solution and coagulation, etc.

On atramenta.

Atraments are either black, reddish, or green; and they are all hot and dry. They are likewise secret and wonderful in their nature. The green atrament mixed with quicksilver coagulates it, and nothing else will bring about the same effect. It also very quickly sublimes quicksilver, mortifies it, and renders it liquid. Believe what I say, open your eyes, and try. The preparation of water of atrament is as follows: Take of the green ultramontane atrament, shake it, place it in a jar, which you should close up with clay; plunge the jar in coals, and expose it to gentle heat for two hours. Quicken the fire with the bellows for two hours longer; then leave it till it goes out of its own accord; allow the jar to cool, open it, and you will find an atrament of an intense ruby colour. Place in a glass vessel; put over it a threefold quantity of clear boy's urine; keep it for eight days; distil with vinegar or sweet water, cover it up, and keep it for use.

On alums.

There are many species of alum. The Jamen variety is feathery, very white, and acid. This is well-suited for dissolving purposes. Hence the Sages have called it the Stone of Stones, because it is neither too hard nor too soft. It is not easily soluble, and is regarded as approaching a vegetable nature. There is another alum which is green, and in the form of a powder; one is of an orange colour, and one is whitish.

There is also a rock alum, like sal gemmæ. But the first is the most useful in our Art. Take of it as much as you want, pound it gently into a brazen mortar, place it in a brazen pot, pour over it six times its quantity of clear boy's urine, expose it to gentle heat: half the urine must evaporate; then remove it from the fire, strain it through a filter, place in a glass vessel, and keep for use.

Alum is prepared with distilled boy's urine, there being one part of alum to four of the urine, in which it must be dissolved after pounding. Then, in order that the operation may succeed, distillation by the filter and congelation must be repeated several times.

To prepare common salt, whence all salts originate, pour over it five times its quantity of sweet hot water; distil it, strain it through a filter, and coagulate. Repeat this operation several times till you have it in the form of snow-white crystals.

Of salts.

In armoniac salt are hidden all the

secrets of the Sages, and because of its soaring nature, they have called it the Eagle, or the Arrow. It is very hot and very dry; yet it is nothing but condensed vapour collected from soot in baths. There is also sal gemmæ, which is more precious than other salts, and very efficacious in our Art. Other salts are saltpetre and common salt. The purer salt is the greater is its efficacy. One salt the Sages have essayed to hide. It is the salt alchali. If you can obtain it, you have all you want.

Take one part of common salt, pound it, put it in a pot, cover it well, place the pot in a potter's furnace all night, take out the salt, pound it, put it in a glass vessel, pour over it some of your water of atrament before referred to, if it be for the Red Tincture, or of the water of alum for the White Tincture. Let this water be twice or thrice the quantity of the salt. Leave it for eight days; that which is not dissolved sinks to the bottom, the rest rises to the surface, floats there like oil, and is brilliantly white. This latter they call the oil of the Sages or the water of wisdom, because none save a philosopher can apprehend it, being in appearance pure water, yet holding therein a crystalline vapour. When this water is coagulated, we obtain a brilliant Stone, which is called salt alchali. Take common salt, cook it, place it in a glass vessel, pour over it three times as much distilled vinegar or clear water, add half the quantity of alum zucharinum, and as much tartar of wine mixed with alum, pound them, put them in a glass vessel, pour over them three times as much distilled vinegar, or clear water; add two ounces of honey, leave it three days; then take what is dissolved, namely, what floats, having no fæces, over the clear and limpid salt, and place it in a small vessel, having a narrow neck. Add to it what floats on the surface of the lime and alum; place them in the same bottle, with the water of salt. See that you have no fæces, which will spoil the work. Coagulate the contents, and you have a brilliant crystalline stone. What has been said of common salt applies to saltpetre and sal gemmæ. The oftener the salt is dissolved and refined, the better.

Of salt armoniac.

Pound it, put in a pot, cover same, expose to gentle heat, pound again, place in a glass vessel, pour over it twice the quantity of distilled vinegar, or clear water; add water of atrament for gold, water of alum for silver, and leave it eight days; skim off what floats on the surface and is limpid, being careful to take up none of the sediment; put in a narrow-necked bottle, coagulate, then keep it and preserve it from dust, because it is clear and white. Afterwards pound it, place in aludel, having burnt common salt at the bottom; close vessel with the lute of wisdom. Sublime in furnace. If this operation be begun at early dawn, the fire, which should at first be very gentle, should be slightly increased at the third hour, and so till noon. Remove it from the fire, and let it cool. You will find the salt armoniac of a pure and brilliant white. It should be carefully shielded from dust.

Of the spirits.

There are three mineral spirits: quicksilver, sulphur, and arsenic. Arsenic is hot and dry, of great virtue and potency, yet lightly esteemed. It burns up all other bodies. There are two kinds of arsenic, one is of a pale white, the other red. The red is combustive, the white is solvent, and useful for the Tincture; with quicksilver it makes silver. It has a fiery nature, and sublimes quickly. This spirit we strive to render corporeal and fixed, in order that it may permanently colour our substance. It has great affinity for vinegar.

This spirit must be cleansed, sublimed, and exalted; then it will do what no man would think possible. Take pallid arsenic, pound well into powder, place in glazed pot, pour over it four times as much clear strong vinegar. When most of the arsenic is dissolved, after three days, place over a gentle fire, steam off the liquid, take it out, place in a dish, wash well of all saltness with pure water, and dry in the sun. Place again in glazed pot, pour over it four times its quantity of water of alum, and let it evaporate over the fire. Put in an aludel, add twice its quantity of common purified salt, close the vessel, and seal it up carefully. Sublime over fire from morning till noon. Cool, open the vessel, and you will find in it a brilliant substance. Place it in a glass vessel, pour over it its own quantity of water of alum, and leave for eight days. Take up what floats on the surface, put it in a small narrow-necked bottle, coagulate, and you will find a crystalline stone; keep until necessary to use, and see that it is free from dust. If you digest this arsenic with milk or oil of bitter almonds, and afterwards with water of alum, it will be very brilliant and beautiful in the sublimation; and then it dissolves very easily. If arsenic be cooked with olive oil, and then with water of atrament, it will be found in the sublimation brilliantly red and easily soluble. Red arsenic, when its ferment is added, makes glad the heart of the Alchemist; but it is not so easily dissolved as white flaky arsenic. Hence you should use the latter for dissolving and sublimation. To sublime with quicksilver, cook in the manner described one pound of arsenic with one ounce of quicksilver.

Of sulphur.

The decoction of sulphur is the same as that of arsenic. But as sulphur has much air, as well as much hotness and dryness, it is not easily sublimed. To effect this purpose, cook it well, and dissolve it; you will then be on the road to perfection. Without the three substances which I have mentioned, there can be no silver or gold, arsenic being best for silver, and sulphur for gold. Some say that if sulphur be mixed with living calx, it can be easily sublimed; but I do not wish you to waste your labour. Know, however, that arsenic is more valuable in the Lunar, and sulphur in the Solar work. Sulphur is partially white without, and partially red within. Of arsenic the opposite holds good.

If you wish to change white into red sulphur, dissolve in red water by pounding, saturation, and good decoction; coagulate into a stone, dissolve once more with red water, again coagulate, dissolve a third time, sublime over a powerful fire, and that which ascends in the shape of a white dust is white sulphur; what remains at the bottom is red sulphur, which transmutes quicksilver into gold.

Of quicksilver.

All sages have striven to make quicksilver remain firm in the fire; but it is impossible. Mix quicksilver with anything, and the fire will instantly separate them again, because it is a spirit, and has been called the cloud of clouds, the father that enriches the son, the eye of wisdom; the pregnant woman that conceives and brings forth in a day. It says to gold: I and sulphur have begotton you; and to silver: I and arsenic are your parents. I flee from the fire, and leave behind all that does not belong to me in the shape of a sediment. I stand firm in the fire, and make all that belongs to me brilliant and pure; I, being coagulated coagulate, being dissolved dissolve. This seeming contradiction I will now explain, and tell you of its coagulation into the red, and its coagulation into the white, and of its dissolution. Let it first be cleansed with vinegar and salt, then sublimed or coagulated, then dissolved. Take it and an equal quantity of common salt, place in glazed pot (after pounding them well in a brass mortar), pour over it four times as much vinegar, and leave it over a gentle fire till all the vinegar has evaporated. Place in dish, having removed it from the fire, wash with pure water, rinse out salt. Take the same quantity of atrament or vitriol, pound together, place in an aludel, and make paste with pure water, or distilled vinegar. Dry over gentle fire, place in an aludel, and carefully stop up the mouth of the vessel with clay. Leave over slow fire from morning till third hour ; let the fire be stronger from third hour till noon, or none. Cool, open the vessel, and you will find it full of a snow-white substance (like camphor in appearance). Pound, place in glass vessel, pour over it twice its quantity of water of atrament, and leave for eight days. Skim off what floats on the surface into a small narrow-necked bottle, coagulate, and you will have a clear red granulated substance. Keep it free from dust till needed. Item: Take 3 ozs. of olive oil in a glazed pot ; boil up over slow fire ; when it begins to boil, throw in ½ oz. of clear yellow sulphur, shake till sulphur melts, remove from fire, and cool. Add 1 oz. of quicksilver, put on fire, leave till all is dry, take out of pot, and place in a vessel well stopped-up with the clay of the Sages. Sublime over fire from morning till three p.m., and what is in the vessel will then be very red. Pound, place in glass vessel, pour over it twice as much water of atrament, leave for eight days, skim off what floats on the surface, place in bottle, coagulate, and you will have a clear red granulated substance. Keep this also free from dust until needed. If you wish to coagulate quicksilver into the white substance, in order to make silver, take quicksilver and as much white lead (cerusa); pound in mortar, place in glazed pot, pour over it four times as much water of alum or of quicklime, leave over gentle fire from six till nine a.m. Take out of pot, pound, place in an aludel, stop up with the clay of the Sages. Put in glass furnace or baker's oven, or over fire, leave from morning till evening, cool, open, and you will find the lower part of the vessel full of ashes. Pound, place in glass vessel, pour over it twice its quantity of water of alum, leave for eight days, skim off oil of Sages, place in small bottle, and coagulate; you will find a white crystalline substance like ice; keep it, and you will soon know its use.

Of gold.

The Sages call gold the product of the sun. When it is perfect, the fire cannot hurt it, but rather intensifies its colour. If you wish to make gold, you must ferment it, or all your labour will be vain. Moreover, the ferment must be pure. Nevertheless, it does not require much purification, since it is in itself sufficiently pure, but it must be prepared so that it may be easily incorporated and fermented, and for this purpose it must be calcined as we will shew further on.

Beat pure gold into thin leaves; then take red arsenic, pound, add a third part of common salt (*i.e.*, one-third part of the arsenic), take seven ounces of steel filings, pound the three together; take a small, new, glazed pot, put a little of this powder at the bottom of the pot; over it place a plate of gold, cover the plate with more powder, and so fill up with alternate layers. Take another glazed pot, put in one pound of olive oil, boil over gentle fire, add four ounces of clear yellow sulphur; remove at once from the fire, stir with an iron rod till the sulphur is melted, and allow to cool. Add some of this oil to the contents of the other pot : simmer over gentle fire, till absorbed ; add more, place again on the fire, and so on, little by little, till all the oil has been absorbed. Then leave it on the fire till quite dry. All this can be done in twenty-four hours. Stop up the pot with the clay of Sages; next morning, place pot among the coals of a gentle fire, so that it is entirely covered, from six to nine a.m. Take pot, cool, break it, pound its contents ; afterwards pound the gold, place the whole in dish, add sweet and clear water, and stir about with your finger. When the powder has settled at the bottom, remove the water (for it is salt) ; add more water, till the powder has quite lost its saltness. Dry it in the sun, or by a fire, place in small pot, stop up with clay, place in furnace for the space required for baking bread. Then rejoice, for you have pulverized and fermented gold. Take that powder, pound well, place in glass vessel, pour over it its own quantity of water of atrament, taking care that it is neither more nor less ; leave for eight days, stirring twice or thrice daily. Skim off the brilliant substance floating on the surface, and put in small bottle. It should be limpid and clear, and if it be so, happy are you. Take equal quantities of the water of quicksilver, as described in the chapters on quicksilver, of the water of salt armoniac, and of the water of gold; mix the three waters in a bottle; coagulate, plunge bottle up to neck in pot full of sieved ashes, place pot on tripod over fire from morning till evening, and that which is in bottle will be coagulated. Break the bottle after it has cooled, take the Stone which is inside, put half ounce of it on eighty ounces of silver, and it will be changed into the purest gold.

Of silver.

Silver, though composed in the same way, is not quite so pure or well digested as gold, and suffers from two kinds of humidity, sulphureous and phlegmatic, or evaporant. Yet silver may be properly purified by fire; but if, being cooked with common salt and orpiment, it grows black, while there is no blackness in the salt or the orpiment, this is a sign that it is suffering from the first humidity. The sign of the second humidity is diminishment in the fire. By purification and digestion it can be transmuted into gold, for its infirmity is of a negative kind.

The following is the best way of changing silver into gold. Between two layers of common well pounded salt, without extracting its humidity, place a thin silver plate in a strong earthen vessel; leave a small opening at the mouth, plunge among moderately red-hot coals for twelve hours. Take out, and you will find your silver plates corroded and diminished in size and weight. If they are white, it is a sign that their first humidity has been consumed, and that they are well calcined and brittle. If they are black upon the outside, some of the humidity remains. If they are not brittle, it is the second humidity which persists. The sign of the elimination of the first humidity is that the silver is not blackened by lead; of the second that it does not diminish in fire. When the silver is well calcined, and freed of its sulphureous humidity, then expose it once more to fire, till it is soft and flexible like gold under the hammer, and is at the same time compact and ponderous. Take equal quantities of salt armoniac, saltpetre, and borax; pound together, dissolve in a little wine, and let it dry. This will render the silver malleable.

Proof.

Rhasis tells us that copper and iron, being of a different and most impure substance, can no more be changed into silver or gold than an ass or a goat can become a man. But copper is of a strong substance, and easily transmutable in colour, of the same weight with silver, and readily mixed with good silver. But it easily turns black, and is very impure. Yet even Rhasis admits that it is easier to make silver out of copper than gold out of lead. If copper, he says, be calcined, cleansed, and dissolved, it will look like gold, but will never become real gold. Hence he calls all Alchemists fools who hunt for bears in the sea, and angle for fish on dry land, as they will make gold of lead, or silver of copper, when they have made a wolf of an ass. Does not Rhasis here seem to characterize our whole Art as a sophistical invention? How is the difficulty to be solved? Well, if you wish to know all, read all—and especially what Rhasis himself says in his chapter on copper. There you will perceive that his meaning appears to be that the ferment of gold and silver cannot be obtained from lead or copper; but he does not really deny that lead and copper can be transmuted.

Of silver (continued).

Take thin plates of silver, five pounds of arsenic, three ounces of salt, and one ounce of steel filings; pound them well together. Take some of this powder, cover with it the bottom of a pot, over that place a silver plate, over that some more of the powder, and so fill the pot with alternate layers of plates and powder. Let there be powder over the top of all. Place on a slow fire, over the coals, pour over it strong vinegar, and leave it from 6 to 9 a.m. Let the moisture evaporate, stop up with clay of Sages, and plunge pot among red-hot coals; keep up a powerful fire for twelve hours. Then open the pot (after cooling), separate the silver from the powder, pound in mortar, wash with clean water in a dish. Dry in the sun. Add to the powdered silver equal quantities of salt armoniac, of sublimed coagulated quicksilver, and of white sublimed arsenic; pound, put in a bottle, pour over it four times as much water of alum, and leave for two days. Plunge bottle up to neck, which should be narrow, in a pot full of ashes; the bottle should be unstopped till its contents are coagulated. Then stop it up, and place over fire for twenty-four hours. Let it cool, and then break bottle; if anything be sublimed up to the neck, combine all together; pound its contents, place in glass vessel, pour over it twice as much water of alum, and leave for eight days, shaking it twice or thrice every day. Skim off what floats on the surface into a small narrow-necked bottle; evaporate the liquid from the remaining fæces, add ½ oz. of it to 20 oz. of copper, and it will become the purest silver. Coagulate the contents of the bottle in a pot full of ashes, then add ½ oz. of it to 250 oz. of copper, 150 oz. of tin, or 50 oz. of lead, and you will witness a wonderful transformation. There is another way of carrying out this operation, but here is the most efficacious, and however the coagulated substance the preparation of which I have described may be obtained, it has the property of transmuting larger or smaller quantities of copper, tin, or lead into the most irreproachable silver.

Of copper.

The composition of copper is identical with that of silver, but it is very impure and ill-digested, burnt, hot, and dry. It is also very porous, and must be well cleansed of its prevailing sulphureous humidity. In its natural state it grows black in the fire, and is burnt and excoriated; it also burns and blackens other metals, on account of its sulphueity. When the purification begins, the flame is more yellow and less black. Its cleansing is accomplished in the same way as that of silver. Afterwards let it be extinguished with vinegar and fresh swine's blood. It should be calcined longer than silver; and it should remain exposed to a powerful fire for three days. The saltness which persists after its calcination you may remove with hot lye.

Of lead.

Lead is generated in the same way as other imperfect metals. It consists of impure sulphur and dark impure quicksilver, of weak digestion and composition. Its blackness and impurity may be extracted by continued digestion. This purgation may be performed by melting and adding to it one-fourth part of Mercury; then pulverise in mortar with an equal weight of burnt common salt, till the salt grows black. Then wash it out with water; pound again with an equal weight of salt, and so add salt a third time; boil it all up in strong vinegar for the first day, till it is the more purified of sulphur and blackness. Continue the operation till the lead is quite pure.

Of tin.

Tin has white and partially impure quicksilver, with sulphur of great impurity. One-quarter of Mercury and a third part of lead will remove its porosity and toughness. But it must be imbibed with rectified oil, or with distilled swine's blood, till its moisture is removed. Its purification may also be carried out, like that of lead, with burnt salt and vinegar. But Rhasis says that gold and silver are evolved out of it with greater difficulty than out of any other metal.

Of iron.

Iron is composed, like other metals, of gross and impure sulphur and quicksilver. It may be changed into steel, but only with the greatest difficulty into gold and silver. It may be founded with ceruse, but is not malleable after fusion. It is most useful in supplying that crocus which is of so great importance in our Magistery.

Extracts of Lacinius from Albertus Magnus, S. Thomas, and other great Sages.

ONLY to inexperienced and superficial readers can there appear to be any disagreement among the different exponents of this Art. From Hermes, who calls the dissolved body a perennial water which coagulates Mercury, down to the latest Sage, they are all in wonderful substantial harmony. The matter of which they speak is the flower of flowers, the rose of roses, the lily of lilies. Rejoice, then, young man, in thy youth, and learn to collect flowers, because I have brought you into the garden of Paradise. Make a wreath for your head, rejoice, and enjoy the delights of this world, praising God, and helping your neighbour. I will now open to you the fount of knowledge, and make you to understand the dark things of this Art.

Albertus instructs us, first, to collect the flowers, *i.e.*, purge the spirits, then to fix them by repeated sublimation in a closed vessel, then to dissolve, and then to coagulate. First we will speak in general

Of spirits.

The transmutation of metallic bodies is brought about by the mineral spirits, whose abundant purity and digestion impart to them great potency of digestion and purification. By a spirit we mean that which has a natural potency in vivifying and rendering immutable. It is surely not surprising that a most highly purified and matured spirit should effect striking changes in the body of a metal. The quantity of the metal is indeed very much larger, but the qualities of the spirit are active, while those of the metals are passive, and so very little can produce a very great effect. In order, however, that spirits may have this power, it is necessary to purify and digest them very highly, to introduce them into metallic bodies, and to make it impossible for them to leave such bodies.

The preparation of spirits is sufficiently exemplified for us by the way in which metals are naturally procreated. In the natural generation of gold, the spirit is sublimed by the mineral heat of the earth. The dry earth, when heated, heats the impurities, drinks up the superfluities, and retains the grosser parts. The watery, aerial, and igneous parts, being more subtle and volatile, ascend upward. By imitating Nature, Art has invented a sublimation through which we purify spirits by means of the dry element that consumes their superfluities. Nature prematurely sublimes some quicksilver and sulphur in the bowels of the earth by premature coagulation into iron, for her own purposes. I, however, who wish to purify the sulphur and the quicksilver, can put off the coagulation until the spirits are freed from all grossness and humidity by reiterated sublimation. Nature, when aided by man, is much more powerful than when left to herself.

Of the purification of the spirits.

The purification of spirits consists in the removal of all superfluities, but without the corruption of essentials. There are three kinds of spirits, mineral, vegetable, and animal. The mineral spirits, again, are properly three: sulphur, quicksilver, and arsenic, which operate naturally in metals, and to which metals, prepared by Art, are naturally joined. Of these, sulphur is the great active, quicksilver the great passive principle, while arsenic represents the secondary operations of quicksilver—but all three unite in the composition of the Elixir.

Sulphur is an oleaginous body composed of subtle earth, strongly saturated with water, and a fat, unctuous, airy humidity, capable of fusion by heat, and of coagulation by cold. It has three humours, two of which are superfluous, while one is necessary. What we have to do is to purge out the superfluous humours, leaving the third indissolubly united to the purified earth.

Take pure and brilliant sulphur, pound small, incorporate with an equal quantity of common salt, cook over gentle fire for two hours, stirring it well all the time, till the mixture becomes a black mass. Allow to cool: take good strong lye, made of plain water combined with quicklime and vine ashes. Pulverize sulphur and salt, boil with lye water over a fierce fire, stirring often, till all the salt is extracted, with the unctuosity thereof. Dry the sulphur, add more salt in the same proportion as before, and repeat the last operation. Reiterate three times, and then sublime in the following way: Boil alum in an earthen pot over a strong fire for half an hour, when it will be calcined Add an equal quantity of iron or copper filings, sprinkle with vinegar, and mix well. With two parts of this compound combine one part of sulphur, and again moisten with vinegar. Dry in sun, or by a slow fire, and place in vessel thus: Cover the bottom an inch thick with the mixture of alum and iron filings, then put in the sulphur, etc., and over that another layer of the mixture. Boil over gentle fire for three hours: stop up mouth of vessel, increase fire gradually till twenty-fourth hour, cool, collect what is sublimed. The fire should be gentle at first and strong afterwards. Take care to stir the contents of the vessel frequently, and let it be well raised above the fire to prevent the compound from getting burned. Repeat the sublimation seven times, till the sulphur becomes quite white, dry, and clear from all humidity of a corrupt kind. The sign of this perfection is a crystalline brightness and brilliancy.

It is fixed and completed in the following manner. Take strong, thrice distilled vinegar; mingle with it the aforesaid purified sulphur, and one-fifth part of its weight of thrice-sublimed salt armoniac. Mingle all with the vinegar in a porphyry jar. Put in a long-necked glass phial, close, plunge in horse dung, till all is dissolved. Congeal into ashes with the mouth of the phial open. Continue slow fire till all is coagulated: then you will have sulphur which tinges, and remains fixed in the fire. With it you can transmute Mercury, Venus, and Jupiter into silver.

Of quicksilver.

Quicksilver is a mineral body, composed of subtle sulphureous earth, mixed with water, which is partly elementary, partly metallic. Its earthy substance must be purged of its gross sulphureous earthiness, and its aqueous substance of its twofold superfluous humidity. When it is thus purified it unites with purified sulphur to produce the glorious Elixir, and the complete perfection of gold and silver, just as the female menstrual blood combines with the male sperm to make a man.

Its preparation.

Project quicksilver on its father, coagulate a little, pound, incorporate with a double quantity of its sediment; place in sublimatory between two layers of sediment; when fully steamed, shut up vessel, and place over fire gradually increasing in strength, The sediment consists of one part of common salt, one part of black or green atrament, and one part of cuperosa. Let it be seven times, or oftener, sublimed with this sediment, till it loses all superfluous, earthy humidity, and becomes very white. At first let it be pounded with its sediment, till it dies. Sprinkle with vinegar or urine. Place over very gentle fire, for it burns easily. Before you open the sublimatory, let it cool, because its vapour is very deadly. However much Mercury is purified by sublimation, it does not penetrate the body of a metal, or remain there, after the manner of sulphur or arsenic. Its substance, though very pure, is not easily fusible: their fusibility metals owe to their sulphur rather than their quicksilver. It is, therefore, necessary to cerate and to loosen. Sal ammoniac, saltpetre, borax, capillary oil, and oil of eggs are the best media for ceration, to which also contrition is eminently needful, for it subtilises parts and causes them to penetrate one another. Take highly purified Mercury with one-seventh its weight of salt armoniac, thrice sublimed with an equal quantity of common salt; sprinkle with rectified hair oil in the place wherein it is being dried. Dry in glass vessel among hot ashes, or in the sun. Pound and sprinkle with hair oil, and again dry. Again pound and make a paste with oil, and dry. The sign of ceration is that the substance flows like wax when poured upon a plate of silver. The above operation must be repeated, if necessary, until this is accomplished. Take strong, thrice-distilled vinegar (to which add one-tenth part of thrice-sublimed salt armoniac); make a paste, place in glass vessel, close carefully, plunge in horse dung, and then leave on gentle fire about twenty-six days; take out, strain, coagulate among hot ashes into a hard and dry mass, leaving the vessel open till all humidity disappears. Test by placing on red-hot iron plate: if it remains undiminished and gives out no smoke, it is properly fixed. If it gives out smoke, it is not fixed, and you must repeat the coagulative process. The Mercury may be changed into Moon by the method described in the section on sulphur. If on this well-coagulated Mercury you place an equal weight of common Mercury with one-tenth or one-seventh of thrice-sublimed salt armoniac, and make a paste with hair or egg oil, and dissolve and coagulate, it will more readily be fixed. To obtain the red substance, make the paste with oil, ¼ part of the aforesaid sulphur, with one-seventh part of salt armoniac, and one-third of lime and red oil (hereafter to be described); dissolve and coagulate as aforesaid. If projected on the Moon, it will transmute into true gold.

Of arsenic.

Arsenic is a mineral body composed of earth and water; it is oleaginous, like sulphur, but having more earth than oil, and containing a more gross and earthy sulphur. Its purgation for the first sublimation is by means of substances which dry up and consume its oleaginous superfluity, which is the first humidity. The aqueous superfluity, which is the second humidity, must be evaporated.

In God's name, take ponderous, lucid, red or yellow arsenic, pound small with an equal weight and a half of iron or copper filings; sprinkle with vinegar, dry, place between layers of its sediment over a fire, till there is no more steam, close up vessel, increase fire more and more till all is sublimed; cool, collect what appears outside the sediment, place between new layers, in each case about the thickness of one inch; sublime as before, till it is white, pure, crystalline, and free from all humidity and superfluity. This may be done by means of five or six sublimations; dissolve, and then coagulate, as in the case of sulphur, whether for the white or red. Arsenic is of less potency in the coagulation of Mercury than sulphur, but it is possible to extract from it an igneous virtue.

How the abovesaid purified Sulphur changes Mercury, Copper, and Tin into Silver.

Take one pound of living Mercury, five pounds of melted purified tin, amalgamate, pulverize in marble mortar with an equal quantity of common baked salt, till the salt is quite black. Wash with water, till all blackness disappears; dry; add salt again, etc., and repeat the process till the salt and the water cease to become black. Add again an equal quantity of salt, cook over a slow fire, pound for an hour till the salt gets dry; when the Mercury begins to volatilize, project and pound as before, until no more blackness appears. Again wash and dry. Thus Mercury and tin are purified of their sulphureous blackness by constant poundings and assations with salt. I myself have found it necessary to repeat the cleansing operation twelve times! Then let both be fused together (*i.e.*, the Mercury and the tin); project into the mass one-seventh part of our prepared fixed and purified sulphur ; hold it there with pincers till it is all dissolved. Remove quickly from fire, plunge in distilled vinegar, and the mass will be found white, soft, and friable. Place it in an earthen vessel, having an aperture at the top for the reception of the vessel containing the matter, which close; place on fire for thrice twenty-four hours, in order that the mass may be well digested by the fire and the sulphur; after a time turn vessel upside down, lest the Mercury should escape the influence of the coagulating sulphur. Thus the whole mass is changed into white, pure, malleable, and fixed Silver. Note that borax is to be preferred before all things in the matter of consolidation and ductibility.

How the aforesaid Sulphur acts upon Tin.

Melt tin, and give it a strong fire, till all the smoke has evaporated; boil in strong vinegar for half a day, strain through a rag, pound with an equal quantity of salt, till it grows black;

renew salt twelve times, as above. Thus Jupiter will be prepared for the reception of the Medicine. Then add to the melted tin one-seventh its weight of sulphur, as before described, holding it with pincers till it is dissolved and incorporated therewith. Tin is rendered fusible and malleable as follows: Put some calcined borax in a saucepan over the fire, dissolve in good wine, plunge in it the lime of tin, boil up till all the wine evaporates; then saturate the lime with swine's blood, blow the fire, and it will presently melt, and be ready to receive the medicine, after the reception of which you will find Jove amiable and well-composed, without harshness, and fit to be the companion and friend of the prepared Moon. The Moon, thus prepared, is first purged with lead, afterwards projected upon rods, ignited ten times, and as often extinguished in swine's blood; it is then laminated, and melted with a little borax, again projected upon rods, set on fire ten times as before, once more laminated and melted. Its purgation is now complete, a tenth part of sulphur is added to it in fusion, and this is the Moon which is the friend of Jove as aforesaid.

How the aforesaid Sulphur acts on Venus.

Take copper prepared in the right way, melt it, add a tenth part of the aforesaid sulphur; it will come forth citrine. Then project upon rods immersed in swine's blood, when the copper will have all the more prominent qualities of silver, and will mix well with it. To change this silver into gold, be guided by the following instructions.

Take sulphur, pound small, cook over a gentle fire in an earthern vessel for seven days, till the orange colour disappears; and you must boil it in refined and distilled urine. Let the fire be moderate, so that the unctuosity may not go forth, but only the tincture, that is, the citrine colour. Remove the urine as it receives the colour of the sulphur, till all has been removed. Let all this be poured into a vessel, and distilled over a slow fire, till the water becomes first orange, and then red. The white water which is first distilled we do not need; distil till you come to the black sediment, and keep that for another purpose. Herein is the Tincture. It is the fire chibric, which is a secret word. Take part of that fire, and distil the water which was first orange, and then red, a second time. Boil the aforesaid fire in strong vinegar, cook over a gentle fire, till the cause of burning is extracted. For this purpose boil till the vinegar is consumed, add to it its dry, prepared fire, make a paste with three parts of the aforesaid white sulphur, adding one part of powdered salt armoniac; dissolve, coagulate, precipitate on prepared silver in the well-known manner, and it will be the best gold.

On Vegetables and Animals.

It has been supposed, on the authority of St. Thomas, that the Stone of the Philosophers is triplex—mineral, vegetable, and animal. Their most approximate matter has never been expressly named by the Sages, but quicksilver has been assigned as that of the mineral, the quintessence of wine for the vegetable, and human blood for the animal. We will, therefore, now say a few words about the two Animal and Vegetable Stones, since those expressions are found in the writings of the Sages, and we wish our work to be as perfect as possible.

Among vegetables, the first place is held by grain, spirit of wine, and salt of tartar; among sensible things by human hair, blood, urine, and eggs. They must be pure of their kind, and then subjected to putrefaction, that so they may be divided among the four elements. After putrefaction dissolve and distil for twenty-one days, place over gentle fire in a cucurbite, collecting the white distilled water in a vessel by itself. The red and yellow water which is distilled should also be collected by itself. Inhumation in horse-dung assists distillation. So continue the distillation till the steam ceases to rise, and only the black and dry earth remains in the alembic. The white water is called water simply; and the red water is called the water of life. Spirits are cerated, dissolved, coagulated, and fixed therewith. The whole water which had the citrine and the red, even to the dry fæces, contains water, air, fire, and oil. To prepare it, place the liquid without the black sediment in an alembic, and distil it over a slow fire. By this process there will be separated first the water and then the oil, which you may recognise by its viscosity, colour, and aerial lightness, as also by the fact that it floats in the water. In this second distillation you will find the fire as something red, black, and dry at the bottom, like the earth in the first distillation. In this way you separate the four elements. The water and oil are also rectified by distillation till they attain a crystalline brightness and brilliancy, without any sediment.

The sediment of the second distillation, called fire, is thus rectified.

Pound, dry in sun, calcine over a gentle fire, till it turns of an orange or red colour, the redder the better. To rectify the earth, pound the dry earth, saturate with its water, dry over slow fire, or in the sun, pound and imbibe till the earth has drunk twice the quantity of its water; dry again, calcine over a powerful fire, add twice its quantity of water; dry again, add seven times its quantity of water; repeat operation a fourth time with seven times its quantity of water, calcine, saturate with a third part of the sevenfold quantity, place in a glass vial, adding a modicum of *bombax*; dissolve in very warm horse-dung for three days, or more; take out, saturate with remainder of that sevenfold quantity, calcine, and it will then be very yellow. By constantly repeating the saturation and calcination, it will at length become very white, and a pearl of great price.

Having rectified the four elements, prepare the elixir in the following way. Dry and pound well the aforesaid earth, saturate with its oil, *i.e.*, its rectified air; dry, make liquid till it flows like wax on a red-hot copper plate; it will then have the properties of silver; pound it with its water, and dissolve in warm dung for three days; coagulate among hot ashes, and you have a most precious treasure. Of this, say the Sages, project one pound upon one hundred pounds of prepared copper, and it will be changed into real, pure silver. If you wish to obtain the Elixir which will transmute into gold, follow the above instructions, but add to the three parts of rectified earth one of fire, and make a paste of all this with its oil, as described; dissolve and coagulate in the same way; project one pound on fifty pounds of prepared silver, and it will be transmuted into true gold.

Hair and eggs must be putrefied under warm horse dung. Do not despise the putrefaction and dissolution of spirits in dung, for only in this way can they be properly digested. Note that the superior spirit of eggs is said to be in the outer shells, and they are whitened by calcination only. They should in the first place be purged from the tela, then pounded and washed in a plain dish, and then placed in a strong earthen vessel with several small openings for the smoke to escape. Set the vessel over a powerful fire (such as is used in glass smelting) for a day and night; saturate with their water and oil till they become fluid like wax, pound this substance with its rectified water, dry, constantly pound and saturate, till it has drunk up its own weight of the water. Pound still, and dissolve in its own water. The oftener the Medicine is dissolved, the more efficacious will it be. To make the metal malleable, ductile, and amenable to the action of the Medicine. plunge ten times in swine's blood, beat into thin plates, lay between layers of common salt and tartar of borax, pound with a moderate quantity of swine's blood, and so make the metal fusible. The same process will render the metal harder if it be too soft. If the Medicine does not enter the metallic body properly, you may remedy the defect with oil of eggs or hair, and salt armoniac. If it enters well, but does not remain, this arises from a defect of fixation, and should be remedied by repeated inceration, dissolution, and coagulation. If it does not tinge well, its purification is at fault; repeat the sublimations, and add more of the metallic body. Moreover, the metals which are to be transmuted, must first be highly purified; and the Medicine itself must possess the utmost degree of purity and digestion.

In order that spirits may tinge permanently, they must first be cleansed, then sublimed, then incerated, then dissolved, and, lastly, reduced to a crystalline form. By means of sublimation the pure is removed from the impure. Bodies are calcined in order to purge out the accidents which corrupt the spirit, and impair the potency of the Tincture. Dissolution is practised for the purpose of permanently uniting bodies to spirits. They are coagulated because powders are more easily used than water.

First dissolve bodies, then form a paste with the proper aqueous or liquid substance, and coagulate in the following manner. Close the vessel, place over warm ashes, leave for two days, till it is coagulated, then project a little of the coagulated substance on a red-hot plate, and if it evaporates, know that your operation has not been properly performed. You must, therefore, add more of the body, and go through the whole process over again. For unless the spirits are bound to the bodies by indissoluble links, they do not endure the test of the fire. Anyone, then, that would succeed in this Art, must understand sublimation, calcination, dissolution, distillation, coagulation, inhumation, inceration; in a word, how to prepare baths, furnaces, and vessels. We will, therefore, briefly describe these several operations.

Inceration.

Inceration is the saturating of a certain substance with some liquid for the purpose of dissolving or more closely uniting its parts, or of facilitating their mixture and purification, as when substances are saturated with a desiccating and penetrant liquid (like common salt) before sublimation.

Sublimation

takes place when anything is raised by air from the bottom to the upper part of the vessel. In the case of liquids, it is called distillation. It is used to make spirits more fit to receive the Medicine, the means being a slow and gradually increasing fire. It is also used to bring bodies into permanent union with spirits. Such bodies are first calcined, then sublimed with the spirits, and this operation requires a powerful fire from the first.

Assation

is to place incerated substances in a glass vessel, and to dry over hot ashes before the fire, taking care to stir the substance from time to time with a wooden stick.

Calcination

is the pulverization of a substance by drying over a fire, and thus depriving it of its consolidating moisture. For there is not a full and perfect mixture of bodies and spirits, unless both are reduced to water which is the first matter of metals ; but this cannot be done so long as they have their natural humidity, which causes them to be melted, liquefied, and moved in the fire, just like water, and holds continuous parts of the bodies in them, and strengthens them so that nothing can be administered to them whereby they can be reduced into water. When substances have thus been pulverized, they are more readily mixed, and saturated with moisture.

Dissolution

is the reduction of a calcined body to water. The body must be first calcined, then saturated with dissolving water, then dried before the fire, then placed in a vessel where dissolution can take place ; whatever still remains undissolved must again be prepared by the same series of operations. Dissolve by making a hole in a damp place, or in a stable, of the depth of two cubits ; fill the hole full of water, till it is absorbed, and also put in some sand. Place in the hole the bottle having the substance to be dissolved; seal up bottle with wax; wrap up the same in straw; cover up the wax with moist sand, leave for seven days, or more, and the whole will be dissolved into water. Another dissolution is by means of S. Mary's bath. Repeat the operation, till it is perfectly accomplished.

Distillation.

Distillation is the purification of water that falls drop by drop, and is performed by means of a filter, or by steaming off a liquid over the fire, and condensing it again. It is also performed by water in S. Mary's Bath.

Inhumation

is the placing of a soluble or dissolved substance in dung for purposes of dissolution (and then one part of the excrement of pigeons is mingled by means of vinegar with two parts of horse-dung), or for the purposes of developing an embryonic substance which has already begun to germinate. Make a hole two cubits deep and wide, where the wind cannot blow nor the sun shine; light in it a coal fire and keep up same for six hours. Take out the cinders, fill up the hole to the height of one foot with plain horse-dung, cover the side of the hole with a mixture of pigeon's excrement and horse-dung. Place in the hole a box, which fill up inside with the mixed excrements; plunge a urinal into box, and over this place a little dish; inside the urinal put the vessel with the substance to be dissolved, leave for seven days, pouring over it a quantity of hot water twice every day.

Precepts of Albertus.

Above all I exhort you to be careful not to make any mistake, first in the pounding, then in the sublimation, then in the fixation, then in the calcination, then in the dissolution, then in the distillation, then in the coagulation. Perform all these operations properly, in their correct order, and you will not go wrong. If you reverse, or interfere with the order in any way, you are sure to get into difficulty.

Therefore Albertus says:—

Know that before I found the truth, I fell into many errors and mistakes; and it was by constant trials, mistakes, and study that the secret was made known to me. I pored over the books of all the Sages, from Morienus, Aristotle, and Plato downward, but yet I went wrong, till by trials and mistakes I at length discovered the truth. For this reason I desired to set forth to you plainly all my discoveries, and I have put down nothing except what I have seen with my own eyes. I have shewn you the hidden treasure which many seek, and cannot find. I have manifested to you what was hidden in darkness, the Holy Stone, which is better than all other things in this world.

*End of the Extracts from Albertus,
S. Thomas, and others.*

Curious Investigation concerning the Nature of the Sun and Moon, from Michael Scotus.

IF we ask ourselves as a first question whether the gold of alchemy be true gold or not, it would appear at first sight as if we must answer in the negative; because gold is properly generated in the bowels of the earth, and therefore, whatever is not so generated would not seem to be gold. Again, the substantial form can be introduced only by its own proper active principle, which is the Sun, but not the kind of sun or fire that alchemists use. Yet it should be remembered that the real question is whether there can be elicited from the Sun and Moon, by an artificial process, any seminal virtue which shall possess the power of hardening Mercury in a moment of time into gold.

Now, in the first place, it is clear that such a seminal virtue can be extracted from gold. Every body, says St. Augustine, contains certain seminal possibilities of a specific character, which will always produce certain given effects, whenever the requisite temporal, causal, and local conditions are fulfilled. God is the only Creator, but whoever provides bodies with certain conditions may produce, through their means, certain well-defined effects. These seminal possibilities are called by some elementary virtues. We call them fermented spirits, because their action is hindered by the impurity of their bodies. But the spirit must be of a mineral kind, and all philosophers agree that the said mineral spirit is not a universal nature, nor yet is it Mercury in its whole substance, but in part it is such. Gold itself is altogether mineral, as is clearly apparent from its weight, and the ease with which it absorbs Mercury. Hence gold contains the radical seminal virtue which we seek; it is developed by digestive heat, and the impulse of an overruling Intelligence.

Opinions on the First Substance of Gold and Silver.

In the second place, some enquirers, who observed the ease with which gold absorbs Mercury, were surprised to find that this Mercury, though highly purified, did not perfect the gold into the Tincture. But those who know that there is no generation except where there is nutrition—the generative virtue being the residue of nutrition—thought of implanting this virtue by nourishing the gold, and thus stirring up its radical active principle. In order that a grain of wheat may fructify, it must die and, by the action of the sun, its substance, which is no more that of wheat than of stone, must be corrupted, and become fit to receive the form of wheat rather than that of stone. In the same way gold must putrefy so as to be reduced to its first matter, that it may become capable of germination. Many have said that this first substance of gold is sulphur and

Mercury. But sulphur and Mercury are metals distinct from gold, and are not found where gold is found. We may rather say that an unctuous vapour, embodying the nature of both Mercury and sulphur, is the first matter of gold. Now, as a man is generated by his father through the medium of seed, and generates a son through the medium of seed, so gold, which is generated through this vapour, generates gold by means of the same unctuous vapour. Hence the Sages have called gold, when decomposed into its first matter sulphur and mercury.

Of the Reduction of Gold into its First Matter.

In this operation we must be quite sure that our methods are strictly in accordance with Nature; or we may destroy the body instead of perfecting it. Now, gold is earthy, and generically cold and dry, though, in comparison with other metals, it may be called hot and humid; therefore, we must look for special difficulties in transmuting it into a humid unctuous vapour.

It must be carefully calcined in a reverberatory fire (so as to prevent fusion), and saturated with strong fiery waters. By this operation the surface humidity is corrupted, and there is generated a dryness, so that it is hot and dry. Earthy dryness, however, is inconsistent with the hotness of fire. Therefore, the first dryness is corrupted, and another more unctuous black dryness is generated. When Hermes says that the Stone ascends to heaven from the earth, *i.e*, is converted out of earth into fire, he means that gold, by means of calcination, acquires the virtue of fire. Earth has dryness in common with fire; hence the conversion is all the easier, and then it once more descends from fire to earth. This latter effect is due to the operation whereby the calcined dry substance, through the mediation of our aerial water, by saturation has its dry nature corrupted, and an airy humid nature generated instead. Again the heat of fire is inconsistent with this humidity; hence it is corrupted and becomes a temperate moist warmth. Our vapour, then, is a substance intermediate between water and air. Thus gold returns to its root, and becomes a vapour, which is called the first matter of the Sun. Hence Geber, speaking to the artist, says in *Med. tert. ord.*, c. 78: You have extracted the precious earth, and so that has come to pass which is meant by Hermes, when he says: It again descends from heaven, *i.e.*, from fire to earth, *i.e.*, to the first matter—and thereby acquires the strength both of things above and of things below. He says that we must extract the four elements, *i.e.*, stir up the seminal virtues, or the active and passive qualities. The vapour which results is called by a countless variety of names.

Why it is called a Stone.

The substance has also been named after all the different varieties of salt, and this custom has given rise to many grevious errors. We prefer to call it a spiritual mineral virtue, as such a designation is less misleading, and implies that the gold has received the power of germination and propagation. But as every spirit is contained in a humid substance, the Sages have endeavoured to convert this spiritual potency, by repeated solution and calcination, into something humid and unctuous. Thus, elementary earth germinates through the frequent irrigation of rain descending from heaven. Thus, also, the heat and dryness of the earth gradually give way to fatness and moisture, as the rain continually ascends and descends. If it be denied that by such means gold can really be converted into vapour, Plato tells us that if it be impossible to convert it into fire, it must then become the next thing to it, which is air. If a figure cannot be made circular, let it be square; in other words, the body must be reduced to its utmost limit of simplicity. That gold receives greater virtue by this process is clear from the fact that one ounce of prepared gold will fix one pound of spirit in one day, or, if the gold has been prepared ten times, it will fix one pound in an hour.

Third part.

Our third question is how this virtue should be sown. The earth in which it is best placed is a mineral nature, because we are fed and derive our growth from the things by which we are generated. What we need for this purpose is a mercurial virtue, and hence it must be sown in mercurial earth. This earth, however, must first be cleared, *i.e.*, it must be purified and sublimed by means of a powerful fire, though all the time its essential part must be kept from combustion. The gentle fire which we need for this purpose, is one that conserves humidity, and perfects fusion. The seminal virtue must be strong enough to fix the spirits which are enclosed with it in the vessel; for so the virtue is multiplied and grows. But if the fire be too strong, the spirits escape and evaporate, and fixation cannot take place. What is fixed, fixes; what is coagulated, coagulates; our substance impregnates itself and is the most wonderful thing on earth. Sow the gold of the

Sages, says Mary, when it has been philosophically prepared, in the earth of leaves, there it will grow, be nourished, and increase, like other plants. When you see that the process of fixation has begun to take place, then rejoice, for you are about to obtain your heart's desire. But as only that sperm which is prepared in the vital liver generates in the case of animals, so only after long and patient digestion are our mineral spirits capable of producing our Stone. While the process of digestion is going on, the vessel must be kept carefully closed, or the spirits will escape; and as the fire must not be powerful, the operations must be frequently repeated over a gentle fire, in order to produce the same effect. When the Stone is once perfected, it may be indefinitely multiplied in quantity; *e.g.*, one part, after the first sublimation, would perfect ten parts of common metal; if it be twice dissolved and coagulated, it perfects one hundred parts; if three times, it perfects two hundred parts; if twelve times, it tinges indefinitely. The solution, says Plato, takes place in the Moon, the coagulation in Saturn: and thereby our Stone acquires the virtue of all the planets. And again: the solution takes place in the water, the coagulation in the fire: thereby our Stone acquires the strength of the elements above, and of the elements below.

As to the fourth question (that of time), we say that those who wish to bring forth the child before the proper period produce an abortion. In order, then, that we may know when the time of perfection may be considered near, it is necessary to observe the signs of development in our Magistery. When the substance is in the white stage, it is more subtle than air, and more brilliant than snow. Not long afterwards it may be expected to reach the red stage. The addition of the orange colour, which is obtained from Mercury, is the only difference between the red Stone and the white. As a consequence, its air is more spiritual, its quicksilver more limpid, its fire more condensed, and its coldness more effectual. The white stage is brought about by constant sublimation and distillation through a filter; the red stage by the intensity of the calcined waters. In the second place, there must be constant solution by means of strong waters, and increasing assation. Then the substance must be liquefied and slightly coagulated. This must be followed by a subtle purification of the whole material. Next you should light a violent precipitatory fire. The sixth operation includes all that have gone before, and perfects the Stone. If you add a grain of the Stone to a glass of sound wine, it cures leprosy, the itch, and all fevers, and purges all corrupt humours out of the human body; it straightens palsied limbs, and conserves youth. He who uses this medicine will always be merry and in ruddy health. Project one ounce upon forty pounds of melted white or red Mercury, and it will at once be fixed and changed into silver or gold. It has also the virtue of rendering gems, diamonds, and precious stones far more precious and beautiful, and of giving them a more intense colouring. The medicinal efficacy of our Stone has been variously explained by the various Sages. Some regard it merely as an intensification of the power of gold to comfort and strengthen the heart of man. Some have compared it to the action of the magnet upon the steel; only both the magnet and the steel are, of course, mineral, while man and the Elixir belong to two different natural kingdoms. It is more reasonable, perhaps, to attribute the medicinal efficacy of our Stone upon the human constitution to the mystical influences which the heavenly bodies exert over both minerals and animals, and the same are found in our Stone in a specially concentrated form. But, however we may explain the fact, let us thank God that it is a fact, and that it has pleased Him to bestow so great a boon upon men. To Him be praise and glory in all eternity, world without end. Amen.

FINIS.

The Pearl of Great Price.

ANALYTICAL TABLE OF CONTENTS.

Introduction. Different modes of Demonstration, 49, 52.

ARGUMENTS WHICH MAKE AGAINST ALCHEMY.

Alchemy seems false because of the proportion of the elements, 53.
The form follows the determinate mode of mixture, 53, 54.
Specific differences, 54.
Objection on account of the instrument, 54.
How Nature generates, 55.
Objection in respect of time, 55.
The generation of anything requires a certain time, 55.
Time of metallic generation, 55.
Local objection, 56.
Local differences, 56.
Internal principle, 56.
Objection on the ground of separation, 57.
Commixtion and corruption, 57.
No transmutation among species, 57.
Specific differences of metals, 57.
Alchemy ignores principles of mixture, 58.
Influence of heavenly bodies, 58.
Products of Art not products of Nature, 58.
Generation of natural and artificial forms, 58.
Methods of Nature and Art, 58.
Alchemy false, because hard to find, 59.
Alchemy false, by reason of contraries, 60.
Contraries cannot coexist, 60.
No substance can act in different ways at the same time, 60.
Objection in respect of the substance, 61.
The first and second spirits of metals, 61.
Tutia, and the requisites of our work, 61.
The nature of spirits, 62.
Metallic fusion, 62.
Vitrificatory fusion, 63.
Vitrified substance cannot become metallic or malleable, 63.

Metallic humour peculiar to metals, 63.
Marcasite and antimony: how not metals, 64.
Glass not fusible with metals, 64.
Metallic humidity, 65.
Vitrification of spirits spoils the work, 65.
Objection: All metals complete in themselves, 65, 66.
Objection. Ultimate disposition of metals, 66.
Objection: Difference of generation, 66.
Objection: Alchemy accidental, 67.
Objection: Accident not amenable to science, 67.
What is fortuitous? 67.
Aristotle cited against Alchemy, 68.
His authority claimed in favour of Art, 68.
Accidents do not change species, 68.
Species and accidents, 69.
Alteration is change of accidents, 70.
How transmutation takes place, 70.
Objection: Specific differences of metals unknown, 70.
Accidents: why known, 71.
Objection: Proportion of ingredients unknown, 72.
Objection: Change into first substance impossible, 73.
Generation caused by substantial form, 73.
How man is developed out of food, 74.
Do metals differ like health and disease? 74.
Differences of accidents, 74.
Whence proper passivities proceed, 75.
Passivities of gold, 75.
How disease becomes health, 76.

PROOFS OF THE TRUTH OF ALCHEMY.

The testimony of Sages is a strong proof, 78.
Alchemy is the sequel and rule of Nature, 79.
Authors of Alchemy, 79, 80.
Theory confirmed by experiment, 81.
In obscure matters use plain reasons, 81.
Objections to Alchemy are ridiculous, 82.
Basis of the best arguments for Alchemy, 83.

ARGUMENTS IN FAVOUR OF THE ART.

Alchemy cannot be demonstrated to the incredulous, 84.
To whom we compare those who deny Alchemy, 85.
How the science of Medicine is demonstrated, 86.
Demonstration of Experiment, 86.

Analytical Table of Contents.

Illustration: divers medicines, 86.
Mathematical demonstration, 87.
The two perfect metals are the two luminaries, 87.
The principles of Alchemy are twofold, 88.
The first principle in our Art, 88.
The tests of gold, 89.
The second principle of Alchemy is Divine, 89.
The gold of Alchemy is true gold, 90.
Their forms are the same, 90.
The best investigation is by accidents, 91.
Properties of gold, 91.
Plato and Aristotle, 91.

THE ART PROVED BY ANALOGY.

A calf generated in the clouds, etc., 93.
Generation of bees, wasps, beetles, etc., 93.
Things generated from putrefaction and by propagation, 93.
Nature changes one species into another, 94.
Sudden causes of generation, 96.
Influence of local causes (bread, stone), 96.
Generation of atraments and smoke of wood, 97.
Metals may be transmuted in different ways, 98.
How Art follows Nature, 99.

A GENERAL DETERMINATION ON THE DIFFICULTY OF ALCHEMY.

Praises of Alchemy, 100.
The subject matter of Alchemy, 100.
Definition of Alchemy, 100.
How Alchemy differs from Medicine, 101.
First difficulty of Alchemy, 101.
Second difficulty of Alchemy, 101.
Sophistic Art is no Art, 102.
Alchemy is true, clear, and real, 103.

EXPLANATION OF THE METHOD OF PROCEDURE.

The Alchemist should be wise and experienced, 105.
Definition and exposition of Alchemy, 106.
Final cause of Alchemy, 106.
While agent acts on substance, a thing is imperfect, 107.
Why gold alone is a perfect metal, 107.
Perfection of metals, 108.

MODES OF THE DIFFICULTIES OF ALCHEMY.

Ten difficulties of Alchemy, 109.
Its supernatural character, 109.
Received by revelation or from a teacher, 109.
Seeming disagreement of Sages, 110.
The paucity of Alchemistic Masters, 111.

Apparent contradiction of the Sages, 111.
The substance is both precious and vile, 111.
Different names in this science, 112.
Alchemist should be patient and studious, 112.
Allegorical style, 113.
This science very different from other sciences, 113.
Difficulty of finding the right vessel, 114.
Time when Stone arises not clearly defined, 115.
He who knows the weights knows all, 115.
Every action has its own proper time, 116.
Why Sages have varied the time, 116.
Secret of the fire, 116.
Substance is tenth cause of difficulty, 116.
Substance of the Stone and its many names, 117.
Metallic substance in Nature and Art the same, 117.
What is least divided is most knowable, 117.

THE UNITY OF ALCHEMY.

How this Art is one, and the agreement of the Sages, 119.
Nature, genus, substance, and essence, are the same things, 120.
Objections, 121.
Difference between body and spirit, 121.
How there is one method and one Stone, 122.
Deceptive operations, 122.
First distinction, 123.
Name of Stone (and Soul) at its birth, 123.
Our Art is called divine, 124.
Knowledge of Alchemy transcends Nature, 124.
By means of Stone the Sages have predicted the future, 124.
viz: the Day of Judgment and the Resurrection of the Dead, 125.
Also the coming of God in the flesh, 126.
Only man could be united to God, 126.
Praise of our Magistery, 127.
The second distinction, 128.
How the Art is found, and to whom given, 128.
Alchemy could not be naturally found, 128.
The book of secrets is really Aristotle's, 129.
Why Alchemy is obscurely described, 129.
Why the Sages spoke allegorically, 130.
The Sages concealed the Art not invidiously, but justly, 130.
This science is not for all, 130.

Manual and ocular operation necessary, 131.
When the 1st and 2nd operations take place, 132.
Theory without practice useless, 134.
Practice more important than theory, 134.
Mistakes corrected by knowledge only, 135.
Ignorance of natural principles prevents imitation of Nature, 135.
Third Distinction, 137.
Agreement of Sages is in favour of Alchemy, 137.
Alchemy only less noble than theology, 138.
The four noble sciences, 139.
Apart from its allegories, the Art is short, 140.
Fourth Distinction, 141.
Second part of the Magistery is the Key of whole work, 141.
Volatility of the Stone at its Birth, 142.
The union of the elements, 142.
At its Birth the Stone needs the Artist's aid, 144.
Illustration of child in womb, and chicken in egg, 143, 144.
The Beginning and end of the Work, 145.
When the beginning is varied, all is varied, 145.
The end is fixation of our substance, 145.

Fifth Distinction, 146.
This science was known to the Prophets, 147.
It enters into all other sciences, 147.
What is truth, and allegory? 148.
The countless names of the Stone, 148, 149.
The Stone being a thing by itself, has no proper name, 150.

REFUTATION OF THE OBJECTIONS TO ALCHEMY.

Refutation of first five objections, 152.
Arts makes the Stone out of Nature's metallic substance, 153.
How far can Art follow Nature? 153.
Fire alone cannot perfect metals, 154.
The Stone is either volatile or fixed, 154.
Refutation of the sixth objection, 155.
How far this Art is natural, how far artificial, 155.
Solution of objection vii., 157.
Opinions on induction of soul into substance, 157.
Answers to objections viii. and ix., 157, 158.
Astrology to be set aside, 158.
How the stars act on the lower world, 159.

DD

Answer to objection x., 159.
The active or specific form, 160.
The accidental form, 160.
The artificial form, 160.
Form of the Stone not artificial, 161.
Natural and artificial forms, 161.
The principle of Art is Nature and man's reason, 163.
The principle of Nature is the Divine intelligence, 163.
Answer to objection xi., 163.
How it is easier to construct than to destroy, 163.
Objections xii., xiii., and xiv. answered, 164.
How nourishment is obtained from all sources, 164, 165.
Causes of metallic diversity, 166.
Objections xv. and xvi. answered, 167.
Metals, why perfect or imperfect, 167.
Illustration: Egg and chicken, 167.
Possibility of development in substantial form, 168.
Objections xvii.—xx. answered, 168.
Answer to five objections of Aristotle, 169.
Alchemistic change real, 170.
How the form is known, 171.
Alchemical Gold is real, 172.
Metals specifically different according to Aristotle, 172.
The potential and the actual, 172.
Not everything out of which something is made is its substance, 173.
Threefold sense of potentiality, 173.
How Nature perfects imperfect metals, 175.
Different senses of perfect and imperfect, 175.
Perfection and imperfection in things possessing the same form, 175.
Perfection and imperfection under different forms, 175.
Third sense of perfection and imperfection, 175.
Imperfect metals are such by design, 176.
How metals are found in mines, 177.
Specific differences of metals, 179.
Metallic digestion progressive, 179.
First substance of man, 180.
How Nature and Art reduce metals to first substance, 180.
The stone is the form of gold in metals, 180.
Objections concerning first substance answered, 181.
First substance or chaos, 182.
First substance and proximate substance, 182.
Order of Nature in the generation of metals, 182.
Time of Nature differs from time of Art, 183.

How the Stone perfects common metals, 183.

Art perfects all common metals instantly, 183.

PHILOSOPHY OF ALCHEMY.

Real existences are threefold, 185.

Real existences have determinate substance, 185.

Divine existences have no substance, 185.

Whence all sciences and Arts emanate, 186.

Nature cannot be false, nor Art that follows her, 187.

The first principle of Nature and of Art, 187.

The substance of Nature and of Art, 187.

THE PRIME PRINCIPLES OF METALS.

In metallic generation there is a twofold humidity, 191.

The first substance of all metals, 191.

The proximate substance of metals, 192.

Some sulphurs are fusible, and some are not, 192.

The first, the next, and the proximate substance of metals, 191, 192.

Nature generates gold in two ways, 193.

Which of the two is imitated by Art, 193.

Whether gold can be made of vegetable substance, 194.

Difference of procedure does not differentiate results, 194.

Answers to Objections xviii. and xix., 195.

Alchemy eliminates corruptive sulphur, 196.

The inward sulphur of Mercury gives the form of gold, 196.

Not every alterant generates gold, 197.

THE GENERATION OF METALS.

Sulphur and quicksilver are as the thing moving and the thing moved, 198.

Separation of sulphur and quicksilver, 199.

The active principle and the end of metals, 199.

When the substance receives the form, 199.

Termination by proper and by foreign limits, 199.

Secret of the operation of the Stone, 199.

Conversion of Elements, 200.

Illustration: Must and blood, 201.

Whiteness when it appears, and what it is, 202.

Names of quicksilver, 202.

In Nature there is one decoction, in Art two, 204.

The Stone is the form of gold, 205.

Form does not operate by itself, 206.

Forms are given according to substantial disposition, 207.

When and why Aristotle denied Alchemy, 207.

How the Ideas of Plato are assailed, 208.

How to investigate truth, 208.

How truth is known in practical and speculative science, 208.

A young man cannot be wise, 209.

When Aristotle confessed the truth of Alchemy, 209.

A DEMONSTRATION OF ALCHEMY AFTER ANOTHER MANNER.

The principal arguments in favour of Alchemy, 210.

Alchemistic gold is purer than natural gold, 211.

First Argument: Crude things can be digested, 211.

Digestion and heat: Their effects, 212.

Digestion aided by outward heat (ripening of fruit, &c.), 212.

How the Regimen of Art and Nature differ, 214.

Can gold become imperfect, &c., 214.

In what respect the digestion of gold and of the elixir differ, 215.

Answer to objection: Crudity of quicksilver, 216.

Cause of imitating Nature, 216.

Atraments, 217.

The natural and artificial production of gold, 217.

When you know substance, and mode of procedure, you can set to work, 217.

Alchemy is true, because possible, 218.

Second Argument, 219.

Third Argument, 219.

To what we compare proportion and mutation of metals, 220.

Why Elements are transmutable, 220.

Metals more homogeneous than Elements, 220.

Elements are mutually convertible, 220.

Difference between transmutation of metals and of elements, 220.

Intellect and Intelligence, 221.

Fourth Argument, 221.

Alchemy is true by reason of intermediate motion, 221.

One thing becomes another in two ways, 222.

Fifth Argument, 222.

AN EXCELLENT INTRODUCTION TO THE ART OF ALCHEMY.

Eight chapters containing the most necessary Instruction, 223.

Chapter First: The substance of the Stone, 224.
Effects of fixed and volatile sulphur, 226.
Operation of quicksilver in the fusion of metals, 227.
Imperfection of silver. Sulphur, 227.
To what substances quicksilver adheres, and why, 227.
Whence the Stone is elicited, 228.
Identity of quicksilver in metals, 229.
Mercury is the root of all things, 229.
Whether sulphur forms part of material gold, and of the Philosopher's Stone, 230.
Colour of gold and tincture of the Stone, how imparted, 232.
Common sulphur does not mix with fixed quicksilver, 232.
The Stone consists of quicksilver and its internal sulphur, 231, 232.
The design of Alchemy, 233.
Chapter Second: Dicta of Solomon, etc., on sulphur, 234.
The sulphur of quicksilver cannot stir itself up, 235.
The virtue and action of internal sulphur, 236.
This sulphur is Divine and has many names, 238.
Third sulphur generated out of two sulphurs, 238.
Living water and oil of sulphur, 239.
Does gold consist entirely of sulphur? 239.
Why there are seven Planets and Metals, 239.
Mercury is the beginning and end of Metals, 240.
Ignorance of the substance is ignorance of everything, 241.
The matter and the form, 241.
The form of gold and the material of the Stone, 242.
Chapter iii. Elements of the Stone and of gold, 243.
Form is extracted from potential proximate substance, 244.
Who can find truth, and operate in the right way? 244.
How operation is investigated, 245.
Two elements are enclosed and two enclose, 245.
The form of fire invisible, 245.
The Elements according to the Alchemists, 246.
All things generated out of water, 247.
Elements when separated are useless, 247.
When water and earth are united, all is united, 248.
Why the Artist should know his simple Elements, 248.
Conversion of Elements, and why they are perpetuated with earth, 248.

Why gold, heaven, and the Stone are not corrupted, 249.
Why the Stone is fixed in the fire, 249.
Only one element in the substance, 250.
The fifth Element, 250.
Chapter iv. The ferment, 252.
The ferment and leaven, 252.
Whence the Stone receives its alterative virtue, 253.
Fermented quicksilver ferments all other things, 254.
The Ferment does not change the metals into its own nature, 254.
Composition of the Ferment, etc., 256.
Union of soul and body, 257.
The body is called form, and the soul, substance, 258.
Saying of Rosinus concerning the Sun, etc., 258.
The Red Stone of Hermes is gold, 259.
The Sun and Moon and white gold, 259.
Occultation of Sun in Moon, 260.
Body, soul, and spirit, 261.
When the first and second Stage of the work are completed: Their nature, 263, 264.
Everything has a proper limit to its digestion (bread and soap), 264.
Signs must be well watched by the Artist, 265.

Concerning the time of Fermentation, 267.
Importance of fire, 267.
Declaration of the substance pure and simple, 267.
Aristotle's illustration of the threefold soul: how Nature generates a bare substance, 267.
The operation of heat in itself interminable, 268.
Elemental heat, 268.
Mensuration of heat, 269.
Fire, an infinite process, is measured by intelligence, 269.
Man—the measure of all things, 269.
Chapter v. Poison and Theriac of the Stone, 271.
The two meanings of poison, 271.
Leprosy of metals, 271.
How the soul is united to its body, 273.
Why the body is called the Theriac of the soul, 274.
Identity, trinity, and prophetic virtue of the Stone, 275.
Of Poison and Theriac in their most proper sense, 275.
Chapter vi. Why it is called coagulum, why male and female, 277.
Coagulum, ferment, body and poison, are the same, 278.
Action of coagulum in milk and in the Stone, 278.

Analytical Table of Contents.

Coagulum is the key of the whole Art, 279.
When the Stone is called female, when male and when composite, 279.
In seeds and in the Stone we have both the male and female principles, 280.
What is the old man and the boy? 281.
Persia and Egypt, and the pregnant woman, 281.
Chapter vii. Analogies of the Stone, 283.
The principles in the generation of the fœtus are two, 283.
When the agent is separated from the substance, 284.
Sperm is not part of the thing generated, but only gives the impulse, 284.
Generation of men and of seeds, 284, 285.
The germ is like the heart separated from sperm, 285.
External sulphur generates the heart in quicksilver, 285.
The outward sulphur purged off, 285.
Victory of male or female, 287.
Effects of sulphur and heat, 287.
Not sperm, but soul, is the real agent, 288.
Sulphur the instrument of active heat, 289.
How the principal outward agent acts, 289.

No stone either from sulphur only or quicksilver only, 290.
They are generated, perfected, and nourished from the same substance, 291.
The analogy of common quicksilver, 291.
All gold is generated, etc., from quicksilver, 291.
Chapter viii. Can copper and iron become gold? 294.
Two sulphurs in all metals except gold, 295.
Outward sulphur is purged out, internal sulphur perfects, 295.
Quicksilver of copper and iron can be perfected as well as that of other metals, 295.
Coagulum coagulates homogeneous substances, 296.

EPISTLE OF BONUS ON THE SUBSTANCE OF THE STONE.

Orpiment contains the three principles of Nature, 299.
Nature does not use sulphur or quicksilver exclusively, 301.
What the third principle is, 302.
Marcasite is not the intermediate substance, 303.
Marcasite is unlike arsenic, 303.
The same substance may receive a variety of different forms, 303.

EXTRACTS FROM THE ROSARY OF ARNOLD DE VILLA NOVA.

Analysis of the chapters to follow, 305.
How quicksilver is changed into sulphur, 307.
How the Mercuries of metals differ, 308.
Silver has white, gold red sulphur, 309.
What metals contain tinging rays? 311, 312.
There is only one Stone, 312.
Whence the Physical Stone is extracted, 313.
No Stone without gold and silver, 313.
The Stone is not perfected from metals alone, 314.
The first and true regimen of the Stone, 315.
Of the perfect investigation of the Stone, and the purification of Mercury, 316.
The first error is haste, 318.
Inhumation of the Stone, 320.
The Second Regimen: Ablution, 321.
Division of Stone into four Elements, 322.
The ablution of water and air, 323, 324.
Operations of water and oil, or the soul, 325, 326.
Ablution of fire and earth, 327.
Cause of ablution, 327.
Third Regimen, or Reduction, 328.
Exposition of the third Regimen of Arnold, 329.
Reduction of water over earth, 330.
Doctrine of Imbibitions, 331.
Fourth Regimen: Fermentation and Fixation, 333.
Commixtion of ferment and sulphur, 334.
Dividing the Elements, 335.
Multiplication and projection of the Stone, 336.
Preserving the proportions of the Elements, 337.
Amelioration of the Elements and Fusion of the Medicine, 337.
Preserving proportion of weight in fixation of elements, 339.
Fixation and Composition of white Elixir, 341.
Reduction of air over White Elixir, 342.
Inceration of the White Elixir, 343.
Composition of Red Elixir, 344.
Multiplication of Medicines, 345.
Dissolution and sublimation, 346.
How to make Projection, 347.
Recapitulation of the work, 349.

EPISTLE OF RAYMONDUS LULLIUS.

Short way of making mineral Stone, 351.
Vegetable Stone, 352.

Vegetable and Mineral Stone Mixed, &c., 352-361.
Notes of Lacinius on the Epistle of Raymond, 361-364.

ANALYSIS OF THE COLLECTANEA OF RHASIS.

Natural objects must be reduced to vapour, 365.
The whole consists in solution and coagulation, 365.
Atraments, 365.
Preparation of Atraments. 365, 366.
Alums, 366, 367.
Their Preparation, 367.
Salts and their preparation, 367.
Salt Armoniac, 370.
Mineral spirits and arsenic, 371.
Sulphur and its preparation, 373.
Quicksilver and its preparation, 374.
Gold and its nature, 377.
Silver and its composition, etc.. 380.
A Demonstration, 382.
Silver, copper, lead, tin, iron, and their preparation, 383-387.

ANALYSIS OF EXTRACTS FROM ALBERTUS, S. THOMAS, ETC.

Albertus on spirits and their purification, 389-391.
Sulphur: Its preparation and fixation, 391.
Essence and preparation of quicksilver, 394-397.
Purifying and Preparation of Arsenic, 397.
Operation of purified Sulphur on Mercury, tin, copper, 400.
Operation of Medicine on Copper, 400.
Vegetables and animals (S. Thomas), 404.
Hairs, eggs, and their operation, 408.
Inceration, sublimation, assation, calcination, solution, distillation, inhumation, 411-414.
Precepts of Albertus Magnus, 415.

CURIOUS INVESTIGATION OF MICHAEL SCOTUS.

Opinions on the first substance of Sun and Moon, 419.
Gold must be converted into a vapour, 420.
Reduction of gold into first substance, 420.
Why it is called a Stone, 422.
Extraction of four Elements, 422.
How that virtue is sown, and where, 424.
Infallible signs of the Completion of the Elixir, 425.
Inward and outward signs of the Stone, 426.
Medicinal and other uses of the Elixir, 428.

JAMES ELLIOTT AND CO.,
TEMPLE CHAMBERS, FALCON COURT, FLEET STREET,
LONDON, E.C.

PRICE TWO GUINEAS.

In two volumes, small quarto, cloth extra, gilt.

The Hermetic Museum

Restored and enlarged, most faithfully instructing all the Disciples of the Sopho-Spagyric Art, how that Greatest and Truest Medicine of the Philosopher's Stone may be found and held.

Now first done into English from the rare Latin Original, published at Frankfort in the year 1678. The illustrations reproduced in fac-simile by a photographic process.

This curious storehouse of Hermetic Science comprises twenty-two choice treatises on the Mysteries of Alchemy, and the composition of the Medicine of the Philosophers, namely :—

The Golden Treatise concerning the Philosopher's Stone.	The Ordinal of Alchemy.
The Golden Age come back.	The Testament of John Cremer, sometime Abbot of Westminster.
The Sophic Hydrolith, or Water Stone of the Wise.	The New Light of Alchemy.
The Demonstration of Nature.	The Sulphur of the Philosophers.
A Philosophical Summary.	An Open Entrance to the Closed Palace of the King.
The Path of the only Truth.	
The Glory of the World, or Table of Paradise.	A Subtle Allegory concerning the Secrets of Chemistry.
The Generation of Metals.	The Metamorphosis of Metals.
The Book of Alze.	A Short Guide to the Celestial Ruby.
Figures and Emblems concerning the Philosopher's Stone.	The Fount of Chemical Truth.
	The Golden Calf.
The Practice and Keys of Basil Valentine.	The All-Wise Doorkeeper.

While affording to the modern student of Hermetic Doctrines an unique opportunity of acquiring in English a representative collection of the chief alchemical writers, this edition of THE HERMETIC MUSEUM claims consideration at the hands of the historian and archæologist as a contribution of real value to the early history of chemistry. The translation is the work of a gentleman who has had a life-long acquaintance with alchemical literature, and has been subjected to careful revision by another expert in Hermetic Antiquities.

N.B.—This Edition is limited to 250 copies, numbered and signed.

Now Ready.

Crown 8vo, printed from old-faced type, on antique laid paper, cloth extra. Price 10s. 6d.

A Golden and Blessed Casket of Nature's Marvels.

CONCERNING THE BLESSED MYSTERY OF THE PHILOSOPHER'S STONE.

Containing the Revelation of the Most Illuminated Egyptian King and Philosopher, Hermes Trismegistus: translated by our German Hermes, the Noble and Beloved Monarch and Philosopher Trismegistus, A. Ph. Theophrastus Paracelsus. Also Tinctura Physicorum Paracelsica, with an excellent explanation by the Noble and Learned Philosopher, Alexander von Suchten, M.D., together with certain hitherto unpublished treatises by this author, and also other corollaries of the same nature as specified in the preface. Now published for the use and benefit of all sons of the Doctrine of Hermes.

BY BENEDICTUS FIGULUS, OF UTENHOFEN.

In Preparation.

Crown 8vo, printed from old-faced type, on antique laid paper, cloth extra. Price 10s. 6d.

Turba Philosophorum.

The most ancient of Western Treatises on Alchemy and the Great Work, the subject of continual reference by all later adepts, ranking second only to the writings of Hermes Trismegistus, and recognised as a final authority in the "practice of the philosophers."

While it has been the subject of innumerable commentaries and of the most pious veneration on the part of Hermetic students, this curious fountain-head of alchemical literature has never been previously translated. A very careful version, containing both of the accepted recensions and the most important of the varied readings in the different printed editions, and in available manuscripts, is now preparing, and a limited number of copies will shortly be issued to the public. The elucidations of selected commentators will be added to the text, and in the introduction prefixed to the work an attempt will be made to trace the history and influence of this archaic *Colloquium Sophorum*.

www.ingramcontent.com/pod-product-compliance
Lightning Source LLC
Chambersburg PA
CBHW032006300426
44117CB00008B/922